Museum Collecting Lessons

Museum Collecting Lessons explains how and why museums meet their fundamental duty to collect. It is the first book of its kind to explore the diverse ways these unique institutions acquire what is preserved and used for exhibitions, programs, publications, and online applications.

The 11 chapters that make up the volume are written by museum practitioners working in art, history, and science museums in the United States, Canada, and India. Together, the essays provide fascinating insights into a wide variety of significant acquisitions and museum collecting initiatives. The authors explain customary collecting methods, including donation, purchase, and field retrieval. Commonly shared acquisition denominators are also covered and include mission pertinence, quality control, the feasibility and legality of acquisition, personnel and volunteer involvement, and long-term retention assurances. The philosophies and realities presented within the case studies shine light on recent debates about who is included or excluded in museum collections – especially when it comes to race, ethnicity, gender, political perspectives, places of habitation, and economic status.

Museum Collecting Lessons reflects upon past and ongoing issues relating to museum acquisition practices. Offering valuable insights about philosophical, practical, and ethical collecting practices, the book will be of interest to aspiring, beginner, and experienced museum professionals around the world.

Steven Miller began his museum career in 1971. He has served as a curator, administrator, director, trustee, writer, consultant, and museum studies educator. For 16 years he was an adjunct professor teaching core courses with the Seton Hall University MA Program in Museum Professions, South Orange, New Jersey, USA.

Museum Collecting Lessons
Acquisition Stories from the Inside

Edited by Steven Miller

LONDON AND NEW YORK

Cover image: © Steven Miller

First published 2022
by Routledge
4 Park Square, Milton Park, Abingdon, Oxon OX14 4RN

and by Routledge
605 Third Avenue, New York, NY 10158

Routledge is an imprint of the Taylor & Francis Group, an informa business

© 2022 selection and editorial matter, Steven Miller; individual chapters, the contributors

The right of Steven Miller to be identified as the author of the editorial material, and of the authors for their individual chapters, has been asserted in accordance with sections 77 and 78 of the Copyright, Designs and Patents Act 1988.

All rights reserved. No part of this book may be reprinted or reproduced or utilised in any form or by any electronic, mechanical, or other means, now known or hereafter invented, including photocopying and recording, or in any information storage or retrieval system, without permission in writing from the publishers.

Trademark notice: Product or corporate names may be trademarks or registered trademarks, and are used only for identification and explanation without intent to infringe.

British Library Cataloguing-in-Publication Data
A catalogue record for this book is available from the British Library

Library of Congress Cataloging-in-Publication Data
A catalog record for this book has been requested

ISBN: 978-1-032-10649-6 (hbk)
ISBN: 978-1-032-10642-7 (pbk)
ISBN: 978-1-003-21638-4 (ebk)

DOI: 10.4324/9781003216384

Typeset in Times New Roman
by Apex CoVantage, LLC

This book is dedicated to the generations of smart museum workers who thoughtfully and with great foresight assembled what now represents an extraordinary international legacy of material evidence about our natural and human universe.

Contents

List of Figures ix
List of Contributors xi

Introduction 1
STEVEN MILLER

1 **Making Sense of Your Community Museum Collection: Strategies for Stuff Management** 12
JOHN SUMMERS

2 **Collecting Our Culture: Eeyou Cree Collecting at Aanischaaukamikw Cree Cultural Institute** 22
AANISCHAAUKAMIKW CREE CULTURAL INSTITUTE

3 **Strategies for Acquiring Contemporary Art: Creativity and Collaboration** 43
JENNIFER JANKAUSKAS

4 **Collecting Period Rooms: Frank Lloyd Wright's Francis W. Little House** 57
MORRISON H. HECKSCHER

5 **A New Museum Builds a Collection: How One Gift Leads to Others: James A. Michener Museum of Art's Acquisition Success** 63
BRUCE KATSIFF

6 **A Museum-Defining Acquisition: The Murtogh D. Guinness Collection of Mechanical Musical Instruments and Automata, Morris Museum, Morristown, NJ** 79
STEVEN MILLER

7	Unpacking the Baggage: The Smooth Acquisition and Transfer of the Lee L. Forman Collection of Bags JODI KEARNS AND FRAN UGALDE	88
8	How We Got Our F-16 Fighting Falcon JAMES WALTHER	103
9	Community Collecting Conversations: Acquisition Stories, District Museum, Jorhat, India ABANTIKA PARASHAR	113
10	Collecting Nonverbal History Documents STEVEN MILLER	121
11	Barnum Brown's Bones DOUGLAS J. PRESTON	137
12	Conclusion STEVEN MILLER	145
	Index	150

Figures

2.1	Map of Eeyou Istchee	24
2.2	Aanischaaukamikw Cree Cultural Institute	25
2.3	Example Acquisitions Proposal Email	26
2.4	Some Examples From the CRA Nemaska Collection	27
2.5	Graphic of Acquisitions by Method and Source Type 2011–2020	28
2.6	Elders' Project Examples	32
2.7	First Snowshoe Walk Ceremony	33
2.8	Loan Withdrawn for Ceremony	34
2.9	Acquisitions From Our Painted Caribou Coats Research Project	36
3.1	Kerry James Marshall. *School of Beauty, School of Culture*	49
3.2	Fred William, courtesy PACE gallery	52
5.1	Michener Art Museum	64
5.2	Henry B. Snell (1859–1955), *The Barber's Shop*	67
5.3	Restoration of Mural by Daniel Garber (1880–1958), *A Wooded Watershed*	71
5.4	Fern I. Coppedge (1898–1951), *Autumn*	73
5.5	Edward W. Redfield (1869–1965), *The Trout Brook*	74
5.6	Bror Julius Nordfeldt (1878–1955), *The Pigs and the Crow*	75
5.7	George W. Sotter (1879–1953), *Untitled* (Night Snow Scene)	76
5.8	R.A.D. Miller (1905–1966), *Rooftops, New Hope*	77
6.1	Sample Exhibit Galleries for the Murtogh D. Guinness Collection of Mechanical Musical Instruments, Morris Museum, Morristown, NJ, 2008	80
6.2	Alan Lightcap Restoring for Exhibition the Largest Pneumatic Musical Instrument in the Murtogh D. Guinness Collection of the Morris Museum. It Features Several Instruments	86
7.1	Drs. Nicholas & Dorothy Cummings Center for the History of Psychology at the University of Akron	90
7.2	Galleries, Drs. Nicholas & Dorothy Cummings Center for the History of Psychology at the University of Akron	91
7.3	Students Preparing and Installing Exhibitions in the Galleries of the Drs. Nicholas & Dorothy Cummings Center for the History of Psychology at the University of Akron, Akron, Ohio	92

7.4	Students preparing and installing exhibitions in the galleries of the Drs. Nicholas & Dorothy Cummings Center for the History of Psychology at the University of Akron, Akron, Ohio, USA	94
7.5	Gallery exhibition opening, Drs. Nicholas & Dorothy Cummings Center for the History of Psychology at the University of Akron, Akron, Ohio, USA	95
7.6	Bag donors with Center staff examining pieces upon arrival of collection. Drs. Nicholas & Dorothy Cummings Center for the History of Psychology at the University of Akron, USA	95
7.7	Bags arrive at the Drs. Nicholas & Dorothy Cummings Center for the History of Psychology at the University of Akron, Akron, Ohio, USA	96
7.8	Storage shelving Drs. Nicholas & Dorothy Cummings Center for the History of Psychology at the University of Akron, Akron, Ohio, USA	97
7.9	Bag, Advertising. Small brown paper bag that was originally made to hold a 45 rpm record	97
7.10	Golf bag autographed by some of the 1994 Washington Redskins	98
8.1	Moving the F-16 on a bright Sunday in May 2014	107
9.1	District Museum, Jorhat, Assam	114
10.1	82C Indy Cosworth Car	124
10.2	John Sloan, *The Lafayette,* 1928	126
10.3	*Yonah Shimmel Knish Bakery*, Hedy Pagremanski, 1976	128
10.4	Installing the Hudson River School Artists Garden	130
10.5	Side Chair, c. 1815	133
10.6	Anna Mary Robertson Moses (Grandma Moses), *Vermont*, 1958	135
11.1	*Tyrannosaurus rex* skeleton, American Museum of Natural History, New York City	138

Contributors

Aanischaaukamikw Cree Cultural Institute (Indigenous region of Quebec, Canada)

Abantika Parashar
District Museum Officer
District Museum
Jorhat, India

Bruce Katsiff
Director/CEO, Retired

Douglas J. Preston

Fran Ugalde, MA
Curator
Institute for Human Science & Culture
Drs. Nicholas & Dorothy Cummings Center for the History of Psychology
The University of Akron
Akron, Ohio

James Walther
Museum Director
National Museum of Nuclear Science & History

Jennifer Jankauskas, PhD
Curator of Art, Montgomery Museum of Fine Art
Montgomery, Alabama

Jodi Kearns, PhD
Director
Institute for Human Science & Culture
Drs. Nicholas & Dorothy Cummings Center for the History of Psychology
The University of Akron
Akron, Ohio

John Summers
Adjunct Lecturer
Museum Studies Program
University of Toronto, Canada

Morrison H. Heckscher
Curator, American Wing, Metropolitan Museum of Art
New York, New York
Albuquerque, New Mexico

Introduction

Steven Miller

Museum collecting is important for two reasons:

- By using human or naturally created objects as vehicles of communication, museums literally objectify a way people can learn about themselves and their universe – who they are, where they are, why they are, and how they got there – or might have.
- The results of collecting define the reasons a particular museum exists and presumably will well into the future.

Museums depend on physical information to serve self-determined altruistic missions. The information *is* their collections. This peculiar operating reality makes museums unique. No other human invention singularly and exclusively relies on pieces of the human or natural universe to serve what in application claims to be a desirable emotional and intellectual purpose. The museum idea seems to have caught on with a vengeance. For whatever reason, museums are popular. Why? Who knows. They fulfill no essential practical needs and are expensive to run. Better to leave the question of their validity to psychologists with time on their hands.

Cerebral contemplations aside, the fact of museum proliferations is obvious. There are hundreds of thousands around the globe. More are being formed constantly. They are of all sizes and deal with a mind-boggling array of subjects. Is there a topic for which there is no museum? In application, the creation, maintenance, and future of museums require all sorts of social, economic, political, educational, and mental resources. Yet – new or existing – the one characteristic all have in common is a first priority to rely on the tangible to discuss the intangible. Consequently, museums by definition need to get, keep, and use objects for a range of evidentiary applications. In these capacities things are static vehicles of communication to be examined, presented, and interpreted in the hope of reifying actual and potential content.

The core purpose of museums to form, retain, and study collections gives that charge an ontological value. The first part of the effort, wisely acquiring things of meaning, is arguably the most critical, and perhaps difficult, part of collection formation. It is not as readily appreciated as it should be.

DOI: 10.4324/9781003216384-1

Exactly how museums get their collections is largely a mystery to people, even some working in them. Exhibition labels credit donors or sources of support in the case of purchases. There are boastful media alerts about new acquisitions. On the rare occasion when a collection loss occurs, be it by theft, vandalism, or natural forces, how and why the item originally came to the museum are noted. Otherwise, most of the time the variety of ways objects end up in museums is unfamiliar. This is understandable, yet too bad. Acquisition stories can be fascinating, mysterious, entertaining, insightful, dramatic (or traumatic), and even amusing.

In working with collections of all kinds throughout my nearly 50 years in the museum field, I am keenly devoted to their formation – but only when done with discipline and mission integrity. The thoughts and actions required to get and sustain meaningful museum collections have enormous consequences. In spite of current controversial noise about collection removals (known as deaccessioning in the trade), the vast majority of what museums have will probably stay with them. To me, this retention commitment calls for focused collecting decisions. It is unfair to burden a museum with things brought in on a whim as a result of irrelevant favoritism, commercial speculation, or to just fill empty space.

At best, deciding what to acquire for a museum can be difficult. Collecting policies rarely provide comprehensive directives. They tend to be quite broad, even academically generic in their wording. Certainly they can help a museum refuse the vast majority of inapplicable stuff people may want it to take. Being able to decline irrelevant collection propositions is of immense importance. Rebuffing a potential gift or purchase can be easily done in a mannerly and informative way. In fact, the conversation can be beneficial for a museum's reputation. It is always an opportunity to explain a museum's mission, and it is especially appreciated if alternative destination options are suggested.

When I was a curator at the Museum of the City of New York, I could easily turn down acquisitions totally unrelated to the city. Yet to be sure, objects do creep in for inexplicable reasons. In fact, that same museum now has a deck chair purported to be from the famous doomed ocean liner the RMS *Titanic*. Since the ship never got to New York, unless the chair was used by a citizen of that town to survive until he or she *and it* were retrieved from the icy North Atlantic, it provides no connective proof whatsoever of anything regarding New York City's history.

Given the importance of how museums collect, I wanted to organize a book that might help the field and any interested member of the general public understand how, why, and by whom museum collections come to exist. To go beyond my own experience, I sought contributors from the museum field willing to tell about their on-the-job acquisition work. I was incredibly fortunate to enlist a wonderful group of colleagues to realize this illuminating volume! My only regret is an absence of discussions from the science museum universe. This is a sad lapse in the general publishing arena, as little is written, online or in hard copy, by and about the museology of natural history, archaeology, or anthropology workers for the field.

To begin seeking essays for this study I announced my book plan on the website of the American Alliance of Museums and invited contributions. Interest was immediate, widespread, and enthusiastic. I am grateful for everyone's input. The revealing chapters illustrate a range of motivations and enviable outcomes. While individual examples contain special considerations and results, approaches all have common denominators. These are enumerated in this and the other essays.

Museums are very practical operations. This starts with their collecting efforts. With the heightened professionalism of the field since the mid-twentieth century, what museums acquire increasingly does not wander in by accident. For the most part, what is owned (ultimately for public benefit) arrives as a result of calculated idealism and logical discipline. To be sure, not everything museums want is obtained, and there are certainly collecting failures. But those are topics for another book. The contributors herein present successful outcomes and should be applauded for their wisdom, diligence, and success!

Deciding what museums should collect can range from easy to difficult. The outcomes described in these chapters illustrate a range of acquisition motivations, initiatives, and approaches. In all cases designated museum staff responsible for final decisions had to think about where, why, and how items met institutional missions, practical realities, and public appreciation. Discussions would mull over building upon existing collection strengths, correcting weaknesses, or establishing a new object identity entirely. Addressing the notion that museum collections can act as proof or prop is important. Is a potential acquisition evidence of some aspect of a museum's subject or simply illustrative?

While I am delighted by the variety of the essays contained herein, as museums move forward with collecting initiatives, there will be new areas explored by practitioners. One, unfolding as you read this addresses information technology (IT) evidence presumably of current and future value for art, history, and science museum reasons. How is our evolving digital universe to be collected, conserved, accessed, and made available for the sorts of uses existing museum collections now enjoy? This is a huge challenge. As someone who is and always has been woefully deficient when it comes to technology literacy, but devoted to museums and museum collecting, I look forward to learning how this acquisition wonderland will be navigated.

Too much of what is written about museums these days comes from outside them or is voiced by people with minimal and often brief inside experience. This is especially true insofar as collections are concerned. Yet the public and special interest groups can be curious about what museums own or not and why. For example, present notable concerns are directed at collections deemed to have found their way into museums in a questionable manner. Media coverage of these includes art stolen by the Nazis during their reign of terror or objects taken by colonizers from inhabitants of land once colonized.

Criticism is also now loudly voiced about the absence of things people feel belong in museums. Two recent art museum collection debates provide excellent illustrations of how collection lacunae are defined and addressed. In 2020 the Baltimore Museum of Art decided to sell some paintings to raise money to purchase works by artists not well-represented in their permanent holdings. These were largely people of color and women. While the motivation was accepted, the paintings to be sold caused such a stir within the community and art world that the museum suspended the sale just a few days before it was to occur. Subsequent fundraising brought in money to buy the art being sought to fill historic gaps.[1]

A similar contretemps erupted when the Newark Museum, Newark, New Jersey, sold art to achieve the same sort of collection corrections sought by the Baltimore museum. In the case of the Newark institution, the sale at auction proceeded.[2] One painting was purchased by a private foundation and is on exhibit as a loan at the Philadelphia Museum of Art. Its destiny remains in limbo.

For practical reasons, in my work I have defined museums as public service preservation organizations that explain subjects through objects. The last word is the focus of these chapters. Collections are the things museums own in an official, and presumably legal, capacity to accomplish their tasks. These things have been made by humans or are naturally created. Objects on loan are not included in this category. The words *collection* and *acquisition* can be used somewhat interchangeably in museum conversations, but the latter tends to be applied more during a collecting process and is prevalent when an institution is proudly announcing a new addition to its collections. Museum collections are usually catalogued in a manner consistent with generally accepted professional practices. Objects are under the intellectual and security supervision of designated employees. Security involves both personnel and facilities. All these measures support and indeed confirm the centrality of collecting purposes.

People or entities who give things to museums are known as donors. Their role is referenced in exhibition labels, on various platforms (hard copy or digital), and when an important gift is announced by a museum. Occasionally donors prefer anonymity. Sometimes a donation is a combination of a gift and a purchase. Museum purchases are referenced as such, though the purchase price may be held confidential. The collecting examples discussed in this book include purchases and gifts.

In the United States museums tend to be private legal entities governed by groups of volunteers. These are usually known as trustees. They serve on what is referred to as a board of trustees. For the most part these bodies are self-perpetuating, meaning they select themselves.

This book does not deal with the purposeful removal of collections undertaken by museums. The activity, known as deaccessioning, can be highly controversial, as evidenced in explosive media attention. While the practice has been happening virtually since museums existed, it gained prominent attention in the 1960s.[3] The museum field has established suggested procedures for its application.[4]

Museums can be avaricious collectors. Knowing about how and why they collect will indicate an institution's core purpose. As object libraries, they strive to offer proof of ideas, events, people, and places. In positing the idea that objects should be of aesthetic, historical, or scientific relevance, museums are seen as places of learning, reassurance, discomfort, celebration, fatigue, diversion, reinforcement, and, on occasion, spiritual contemplation.

To a degree, museums have embraced, or been forced to assume, roles once mostly associated with temples, casinos, monasteries, schools, cathedrals, amusement parks, shrines, or sports stadia. Shifting audiences towards museums and away from previously well-established places of learning, entertainment, religion, or public assembly was gradual until the mid-twentieth century. It then accelerated rapidly. Museums have moved from cosseted retreats to mainstream attractions. This reality was expressed most recently by the founder of the new Museum of American Arts & Crafts Movement (MAACM), a new museum in St. Petersburg, Florida. Rudy Ciccarello, a local businessman, philanthropist, and collector of these decorative and fine arts from the late nineteenth and early twentieth centuries established the Two Red Roses Foundation to promote an understanding of the American arts and crafts movement through the acquisition, conservation, preservation, exhibition, and interpretation of those objects. In explaining the museum as a local attraction, he notes it will offer

> the amenities that the museum-going public expects these days. "I wanted the museum to offer guests a unique and entertaining experience and have paid great attention and detail to providing them wonderful amenities. Visitors can relax and have a quick bite or lunch at the Arts Café, browse the MAACM Store, dine in the soon to open Ambrosia Restaurant, hold a special event, wedding or conference in the banquet space with adjoining art filled collector's gallery and antique bar, take a class in one of our studios, or just relax on a bench in our beautiful outdoor green space surrounded by period fountains."[5]

Museum Collecting Lessons is the first book of its kind written by those who have actually made museum collecting decisions. Moreover, it includes a great assortment of institutions. From responding to unanticipated opportunities to accomplishing carefully calculated long-term goals, the examples provide a wealth of thoughtful and practical insights. Essays shed light on processes that can be short and sweet, simple or complicated, obvious or obscure, idiosyncratic or logical, serendipitous or anticipated. One contribution, for the American Museum of Natural History, falls outside my desire to only include actual collecting activities. It is the exception that proves the rule as it describes an essential historical accomplishment and was written by an employee of the museum holding the collections described.

Museums tend to specialize in three areas of academic disciplines: art, history, or science. Methods of collecting vary according to a museum's acquisition interests and abilities over time. Most of what we see in art and history museums has been donated. Purchases occasionally happen. This is also the case for science technology museums. However, when science museums focus on natural history, anthropology, and archaeology, much of the collecting is done through field retrievals.

Regardless of institutional type, there are several common questions museums ask themselves when collecting. Some are obvious. Others are more obscure. They start with the *why* of a potential acquisition. Does the item intellectually fit – precisely – a museum's mission? If the answer is yes, the next questions involve a host of related philosophical and practical concerns. Can the museum keep and care for the object? Does the item have important scholarly value? Does something fill knowledge (read collection) gaps, or is the museum already well-represented by what is being considered for acquisition? How will an object align with what the museum already owns? Are there legal issues about ownership? Does an acquisition hold problems relating to actual or perceived moral, ethical, or cultural debates? Will there be restrictions on how the acquisition can be used and, if so, does that matter? Is an item safe to acquire? (This might be a concern with toxic substances, certain armaments, or art made of or containers holding dangerous chemical compounds.) Will the acquisition process or outcome involve actual, potential, or perceived conflicts of interest? Will controversy accompany the acquisition and, if so, why, does it matter, and how can the museum respond? Finally, if it is a donation, purchase, field retrieval, or some combination thereof, does that present concerns?

What is a collection? Characteristics of museum collections that differentiate them from other sorts of collections include the following:

1. Museum collections consist of more than one object.
2. The objects have order and organization.
3. The objects are valued by people.
4. The objects are collected with the intent to preserve them over time.
5. The collections serve the institutional mission and goals.
6. The integrity of each object and its associated information are paramount to the museum.
7. The collections are maintained in adherence to professional standards.[6]

The first chapter, by John Summers, adjunct lecturer with the Museum Studies Program at the University of Toronto, Canada, gives us a comprehensive review of museum collecting concerns, as well as the importance of how these are, or should be, managed. Getting collections is the first step in a museum's stewardship duty. Everything else museums do flows from what is accomplished by this.

Recognizing that a museum collecting focus can change, the second chapter celebrates how museum acquisition priorities can be radically altered when unprecedented, more inclusive, expansive, and participatory decision-making processes are put in effect by the people a museum represents. The chapter does not have a single author but is collaboratively written by the Aanischaaukamikw Institute, which is in the Cree Cultural Institute. It explains acquisition processes and philosophies of the Ouje-Bougoumou and within Eeyou Istchee, a self-governing region in Quebec, Canada. The independent stance provides an ideal reference for decolonizing efforts now demanded, finally, of European and Western Hemisphere museums that hold items of cultural importance for the peoples from whom the things were gotten either against their will or without their true assent – or not collected by and for them at all.

Chapter 2 reflects a movement in museums to counter collecting done by countries that once colonized large swathes of the globe. Decolonizing the museum is a phrase that applies to a growing practice to address what museums in Europe and North America in particular own that was taken by force or unknowingly from peoples who either had no interest in relinquishing the things, were duped into doing so, or it happened without their willing participation. In application decolonizing is implemented largely through the return of museum collections to their places of origin. While the subject is of immense importance and will grow in impact, it falls outside the direct topic of this book. Some have referred to it as a form of deaccessioning.[7]

Art museums are now subject to severe complaints that their collections reflect a largely white, male, privileged societal perspective. The problem is entrenched.[8] Widespread efforts are underway to correct what is seen as egregious cultural myopia. Seeking more diverse, inclusive collections representing a broad range of racial, gender, political, economic, and demographic visual perspectives and origins is underway. Chapter 3 illustrates how progress can be made.

The vast majority of art and history museum collections are donated. Reasons for this vary greatly but are largely financial. Museums have limited (or zero) cash reserves to buy things. This chapter describes how a smaller museum collaboratively developed two innovative acquisition models to successfully deal with an expensive commercial market. Jennifer Jankauskas, PhD, curator of art, Montgomery Museum of Fine Arts, Montgomery, Alabama, highlights how a sister institution in the South, the Birmingham Museum of Art, Birmingham, Alabama, seeks to collect art by underrepresented or totally absent artists of merit, the vast majority of whom are nonwhite, female, and absent existing academic canons. One way the museum deals in the commercial market for such art is with internal budget reallocations for collection purchases, external funding appeals, and an intermuseum collaboration. While joint purchases are a sometime occurrence, given the financial operating realities museums face and the challenges of successful engagement with the commercial art market, the sort of venture described in this chapter may become commonplace.[9]

Dr. Jankauskas's essay is followed by an example of what can happen when a make-or-break purchase deadline looms for a highly desirable acquisition. In such cases, to be successful, if funding is needed and there is a reasonable chance it can be gotten, museum deliberations need to happen quickly. Morrison H. Heckscher, when he was curator of the American Wing of the Metropolitan Museum of Art in New York City, tells of just such a circumstance. The story is reprinted from *The Chase, The Capture: Collecting at the Metropolitan (1975)*, a book about various acquisitions that the museum's curatorial departments made. While of interest, the chapters in the book dwell more on the art historical value of an item than how it was acquired. This essay is the exception, which is why it is included.

The Heckscher chapter confirms an essential museum collecting reality. Those who have something a museum wants usually must believe in the institution if they are to be successfully approached for a donation or purchase. Judgments by owners rest on assurances regarding professional operations, staff capabilities, governance commitment, and fiscal health. Even what might appear to be an unemotional commercial transaction sometimes only happens with an owner who will only sell to a place he or she likes. The failure of the acquisition of the Frank Lloyd Wright room could have happened because the sellers disliked the museum wanting to purchase it. Fortunately, that was not the case.

Collections define museums. The majority of objects so judiciously assembled over time comprise, in part or in whole, the signature elements of an institution. Think of a museum, and one or more of its acquisitions could pop into your mind's eye. For the Louvre it might be the *Mona Lisa*. The Smithsonian Institution has the Wright brothers' original, and the world's first successful, airplane. Chicago's Field Museum of Natural History boldly shows off "Sue," the world's most famous *Tyrannosaurus rex* skeleton.

But how does a museum become known for a particular collection or collection focus? It starts with an idea of what should or will be acquired. This usually accords with an institution's founding purpose. In Chapter 5 we read about the creation of a signature collection obtained to define a new museum. As the founding director of the James A. Michener Art Museum, Doylestown, Pennsylvania, Bruce Katsiff was charged with acquiring the most significant collection of art that celebrated a famous American art movement in that region during the early decades of the twentieth century.

The museum's acquisition timing was fortuitous. Catalyzing the daunting goal was the unexpected possibility of obtaining a huge painting by one of the preeminent artists of the historic era. Getting it led in turn to the successful donation of a remarkable private collection of work by the masters of that creative period.

Building on the Michener story, in the following chapter, I explain how a significant acquisition can radically alter a long-standing museum's collection reputation. As executive director of the Morris Museum, Morristown, New Jersey, I had the extraordinary good fortune to acquire an outstanding collection of mechanical musical instruments and automata. There is no similar holding in size or scope in the Western Hemisphere. The museum's existing collections, though well cared for, were haphazard and unfocused – consequently, the museum had no collection identity and thus no clear content mission. Today it is internationally recognized for these extraordinary objects that tell about the start of mechanized entertainment that so inundates us today. I am frank in discussing how easily we might have failed to obtain the collection. I also note a poor financial decision made by the board of trustees that was, in their minds, prompted by but completely unrelated to, the gift:

> The point of collections and museums, it is no exaggeration to say, revolves around the possession of "real things: and . . . it is essentially that which gives museums their unique role.[10]

As I noted in the beginning of this introduction, museums for all sorts of subjects exist. Evidence of this can now be found in Akron, Ohio. One of the most unusual museum acquisitions to be made lately is a huge collection of bags now at the University of Akron. Chapter 7 tells how this happened. Jodi Kearns, PhD, is the director, and Fran Ugalde, MA, is the curator of the Lee L. Forman Collection of Bags at the Drs. Nicholas & Dorothy Cummings Center for the History of Psychology at the Institute for Human Sciences & Culture, the University of Akron. There are nearly 12,000 bags of all descriptions in the collection. They touch on just about every utilitarian bag application imaginable, be it mundane or exceptional. Few museums think of preserving this sort of commonplace ephemeral material. A bag or two might be acquired either as part of a larger collection or almost by accident. Potential applications for objects in the collection seem unlimited, especially insofar as delving into the psychology of commercial bag design. What makes this collection of more practical value is its use for teaching at the university's museum studies program

Differences between public and private collecting are readily apparent for James Walther, director of the National Museum of Nuclear Science & History in Albuquerque, New Mexico. His account of acquiring an F-16 fighter jet touches on roles volunteers can play when well-instructed and adhering to a museum's collecting goals. The successful logistics of getting, transporting, and restoring the plane are impressive to say the least! The director must be applauded for his perseverance in overcoming entrenched, somnolent, and counterproductive military bureaucracies.

For art and history museums, collecting can be a highly nuanced mating dance or an encounter quickly consummated. To be sure, success is not always guaranteed. (In fact, another book could be written about failed collecting attempts.) Convincing people to engage with a museum regarding acquisitions is often a process of persuasive cultivation. For those working on behalf of a museum, it requires mission conviction and the ability to convey that. Chapter 9 offers insights about community collecting on a broad scale. Abantika Parashar, district museum officer, District Museum, Jorhat, India, understands the sensitivities of the people whose cultures her museums strive to acquire with care and understanding. There is much conversation in the international museum world today about how things were obtained in the past from Indigenous cultures. Any mindfulness regarding owners was often lacking. Ms. Parashar rejects such abrasive collecting. Her success in acquiring newly excavated items for her museum certainly relied on diplomatic skills once rarely applied for most collecting work. Indeed, she was able to not only defuse face-to-face opposition situations about to turn violent by inhabitants unwilling to relinquish objects but she was able to change their minds. Her deft personal courage and commitment caused them to actually champion the idea of museum collecting for the common good.

The totality of what has been brought into museums over the years is breathtaking. There must be trillions of things in museums around the globe. The general public knows museums through the connective medium of the gallery exhibit. Accordingly, most people believe that is why museums collect. With this perception comes the notion that what is not seen languishes in storage unappreciated and unused by museum staff and visitors. This is a woefully incorrect assumption. In Chapter 10 I discuss a documentary approach regarding acquisitions made in four different history museums where I have worked. The items cited may not always, or even often, be on exhibit but presumably they have evidentiary value for a particular museum's mission. The examples support the analogy of the museum as research library. To this end I am fond of referencing libraries when people express bewilderment that so much of what a museum owns is not on exhibit. In addition to the practical reasons most collections cannot or should not be exhibited always, I declare: "No one walks into a research library and is shocked to see the shelves filled with so many books not being read."

Exhibits are just one of many outcomes of museum collecting. The objects in these institutions are three-dimensional documents. When acquired with care and meaning, they hold information that is obviously known and no doubt will continue to be deciphered over time with further research. In fact, the idea of keeping things "in perpetuity" is probably the most unusual charge museums assume. A sense of this assignment is readily understood when looking at the dinosaur collections of the American Museum of Natural History, in New York City. Chapter 11 explains how one person virtually singlehandedly acquired the core of those holdings when the museum had none. The story is told by Douglas J. Preston, a long-time employee of the museum, who permitted its use in this volume. He provides an excellent look at that incredible museum's rich collection of fossils, for which it is justifiably famous. These signature specimens hold long-term retention prospects for scholarly discovery and public edification.[11]

> There is no reason, however, to believe that collecting will cease or slow down; the pressure for quantitative perfection is still too strong.[12]

As neurological research unfolds about the visceral and cerebral meaning of objects, the rest of us accept the role some items can play in illuminating the past or present human and natural condition. Religions aside, museums increasingly help us seek answers to what makes the universe tick and why. Individuals we entrust to provide such information in museums are still called curators, or a variant of that. These cultural soothsayers decide what tangible aspects of our life circumstances can or should be collected to shed light on the intangible aspects of those circumstances. Private collectors embrace this thinking, but not for public benefit. Nor does the marketplace for what museums collect reflect philanthropic motives. Only museums hold this agency. Naturally curators have strengths and weaknesses in collecting prejudices. This is why over time the value of acquisitions will no doubt ebb and flow. Given the relatively short history of museums, vetting collections will increase substantially going forward.

Museums are odd places. No other public invention exists to acquire things for their mental and emotive value *with the idea of preserving their material content for the long term*. The notion of collection retention forever is a bit bizarre, if not completely unrealistic. Yet few museums flat out reject the idea. Who can predict the future? Maybe someday somebody in some way will figure out how to preserve art, historic artifacts, and scientific specimens eternally. Stranger things have happened.

Introduction 11

"These are issues which affect existing collections but which need to be considered in the formulation of a collecting strategy. At its simplest level object acquisition must meet the need for multifaceted use in the future."[13]

Needless to say, building a collection is a complex and major financial and ideological undertaking, rife with difficult decisions.[14]

Museum Collecting Lessons reflects my personal affinity for museum acquisitions. It has always been the favorite part of my work over the years. I hope this book provides insights into why museums collect and the many ways that can unfold – be it predictable, unpredictable, or some combination thereof. The essays offer wonderful examples of how objects land in museums. I am deeply indebted to the contributors for their willingness to share their remarkable experiences.

Notes

1. www.artnews.com/art-news/news/baltimore-museum-of-art-deaccession-called-off-sothebys-1234575295/
2. https://news.artnet.com/art-world/newark-museums-plan-deaccession-sothebys-1966696
3. www.nytimes.com/1972/02/27/archives/very-quiet-and-very-dangerous.html
4. There are several books about deaccessioning and a myriad of articles, essays, procedural directives, and the like from museum membership organizations, as well as individual museums. It is a subject I have specialized in and continue to find absorbing. I recommend these books for information: Steven Miller, *Deaccessioning Today*, Rowman & Littlefield, 2018; Peter Davies, ed. *Museums and the Disposals Debate*, MuseumsEtc., 2011; Martin Gammon, *Deaccessioning and Its Discontents*, MIT Press, 2018; Stephen E. Weil, *A Deaccession Reader*, American Association of Museums, 1997.
5. W.A. Demers, 'Museum of the American Arts & Crafts Movement', *Antiques and the Arts Weekly*, 24 September 2021, p. 32.
6. John E. Simmons, *Things Great and Small: Collection Management Policies,* Rowan & Littlefield, Lanham, MD, 2018, pp. 2, 3. Quoted from: E.G. Nicholson and S.L. Williams, 'Developing a Working Definition for the Museum Collection', *Inside Line*, Texas Association of Museums (Fall 2002), pp. 1–4.
7. www.museumnext.com/article/what-does-it-mean-to-decolonize-a-museum/
8. www.artsy.net/news/artsy-editorial-study-85-artists-museum-collections-white-87-male
9. www.artnews.com/art-news/news/art-museum-joint-acquisitions-collaborations-1234604356/
10. Susan M. Pearce, *Museums, Objects, and Collections: A Cultural Study,* Smithsonian Institution Press, Washington, DC, 1992, p. 24.
11. Douglas J. Preston, *Dinosaurs in the Attic: An Excursion into The American Museum of Natural History*, St. Martin's Press, New York, 1986, pp. 65–72.
12. Simon J. Knell, ed., *Museums and the Future of Collecting;* Ashgate, Aldershot, UK and Brookfield, VT, 1999, p. 194.
13. Ibid, p. 8
14. Kyung An and Jessica Cerasi, *Who's Afraid of Contemporary Art? An a to z Guide to the Art World,* Thames & Hudson, New York, 2017, p. 87.

1 Making Sense of Your Community Museum Collection

Strategies for Stuff Management

John Summers

A Stroll Through Storage

It is day two of your new job as curator of a community museum. Yesterday was a whirl of activity: meeting the board, lunch with the chair, getting keys and an alarm code, finding your desk and the coffee pot, meeting the rest of the staff (it did not take long because there are only three of you!), and dropping in on the volunteers during their weekly coffee and donuts session at the diner down the street. Today, you are getting a tour of collections storage.

In the lobby, you meet the program coordinator, who is holding a large bundle of keys with a tag that reads "Curator's Keys! Do Not Touch!" With a palpable sense of relief (because she has been acting curator as well as doing her own job for the past three months) she hands you the keys and says, "These are yours now, follow me." You put the keys in your pocket and walk through the galleries to the first of the museum's three collections storage areas. You unlock the door and she says, "Wait here" before walking through the darkened room to a light switch on the far side.

The lights come on to reveal a low-ceilinged room that is crossed by sprinkler pipes and made even lower by suspended fluorescent light fixtures. In front of you are several ranges of shelving holding more ceramic crocks and wooden carpenter's tools than you have ever seen in one place before. To the left, the shelves hold wide flat boxes full of textiles. Beyond that, banker's boxes are stacked six high along the wall. At the back of the room is a life-size fiberglass cow standing next to a tall-case clock.

To the right are more shelves. You can see rows of shoes, teapots and teacups, and children's toys. There is a cardboard box labeled "buttons" and another on which someone has crossed out "children's bedroom" and written "assorted silverware." On the lowest shelf are several ship models. At the back of the room, next to the cow, is a jumble of bicycles, children's wagons, tricycles, and an old gas pump. A large circular metal sign reading "Fire Chief" leans against the back wall. Tilting stacks of banker's boxes line the wall on the other side too.

After a quick walk-through, you lock the door and follow her to the second storage area, located in the basement of the old town hall a few blocks down the street. You go down narrow stairs with a sharp turn to a basement room filled with

DOI: 10.4324/9781003216384-2

the hum of the furnace. Next to a hot water heater is a door marked "museum." Inside are more shelves packed from top to bottom and sagging slightly under the weight of innumerable glass insulators and dairy bottles. Next to these are a stack of thin wooden boxes which, upon closer examination, contain thousands of small pieces of lead type. To your right are tall narrow plywood shelves containing tightly packed pieces of art. You can just see the first one, which shows several dogs seated around a table playing cards.

Having seen enough, you lock up and go to the third and final storage area. It is a rented unit at the local self-storage, located a five-minute drive away on the highway leading out of town. With difficulty, you unlock and raise a dented garage door. Spiders and what might have been a mouse run for cover as soon as the door is raised. Inside, packed so tightly that you could walk across the room on them without touching the floor are carriages, wagons, sleighs and cutters, wardrobes, and other substantial pieces of wooden furniture. Along one side is a large millstone mounted in a concrete base and several pieces of what look like factory machinery. Along the other are portions of several carved sandstone columns from the old Masonic Hall. Some of the wagons contain upholstered sofas and other items of furniture. You don't go in farther than the doorway because, as the program coordinator points out, it will take at least an hour to pull the first three carriages out into the parking lot just to get to the light switch.

Returning to the museum, you are shown the area where the collections volunteers have been working. The wall above the desk is filled with shelves of binders. To one side are several filing cabinets, and two antiquated computers sit on the desk. You are told that the cataloguing volunteers come in Tuesday and Thursday mornings and that they are gradually transferring the paper records into the computer. They have been working on this for the last five years and have made it as far as accessions from 1973. It is day two, and your museum collections journey has begun. All this stuff is now your stuff.

Everything I have described here is taken from experiences gained as a volunteer, staff member, or consultant working at museums in both the United States and Canada. Do any of these issues sound familiar to you? Do all of these issues sound familiar?

In its current condition, this is a collection that makes no sense. It is of little use to the museum, staff, or public. It is more of a liability than an asset, and at the present rate of documentation progress, it will continue to be so forever. With problems everywhere you look, it is hard to know where to start. As daunting as it seems, however, the alternative to doing something, which is to do nothing, is far worse, so you need a plan.

In this chapter I am going to walk you through four simple questions that can help you turn your collection from a liability into the asset that it should be. They are:

1. What do we have?
2. Why do we have it?

3. What should we do with it?
4. Where do we go from here?

By asking and answering these questions, you will come to understand the current state of your collection, think about how you got into this situation, make a plan for how to deal with it, and ensure it doesn't happen again.

What Do We Have?

In more than three decades of work in this field, I have yet to see a museum that was either completely on top of, or even satisfied with, the state of its collections management documentation. In smaller institutions especially, there are often several generations of numbering schemes, and considerable time, and possibly also money, is being spent trying to reconcile them with each other. As new acquisitions are made and collections tasks are pushed aside by other priorities, the backlog of unprocessed items and unreconciled records continues to grow until it just becomes an accepted fact that you will never catch up.

From the early years of the museum, there might be one or more handwritten ledgers. This is the old-school way to keep track of artifacts. Each line in the ledger records the donation date, the name and possibly address of the donor, and what was donated. If you are lucky, it will say something like "three sad irons, two earthenware mixing bowls and one set of copper measuring cups." If you are really lucky, the ledger will also be neatly written in the kind of penmanship most of us can only dream of today. If you are not so lucky, it will just say "miscellaneous household items." Either way, this is often the only record of the collection that covers that period.

At some point, incoming donations likely got ahead of this ledger and began to accumulate. The museum might have gotten a grant to hire summer students to address the cataloguing backlog. Using hard-copy inventory forms, they set to work full of good intentions but by the end of the summer they had only made it partway through. More students were hired the following summer, but it was hard to tell where work on the first project had started and stopped, so they began with a different year and also did not complete their project by the end of the summer. Because everyone was focused on this project, no one updated the old ledger with that year's accessions and so it got further out of date.

A previous curator developed their own numbering system using two-letter prefixes before the accession date to indicate what kind of artifact it was: VE for vehicle, FR for furniture, TO for tools, and so on. That curator has long since retired, but the numbers remain in use. The year that the museum acquired its first computer, one of the board members, who owned an accounting firm, developed a spreadsheet application for cataloguing, and staff and volunteers began to transfer written records onto the new system. As with earlier efforts, however, this was never completed for the entire collection. All those computerized records are stored on floppy disks and a magnetic tape drive, and there is no longer a computer in the building that can read them.

Here is the main problem: none of these efforts has ever made it all the way through the collection, and they each started from a different place. When you put all the information contained in them together, it still does not add up to the entire collection. The best thing to do at this point is not to launch another cataloguing project or hire more summer students. What your museum needs most is a simple, plain-vanilla collections inventory. Picture your collection as a layer cake. Previous documentation efforts have produced what you serve someone after dinner: a triangular piece. It contains a portion of all the layers in the cake from top to bottom but only affects part of the whole. The next person who wants a slice might cut an adjacent triangle, but they could just as easily cut a new piece on the other side. An inventory, by comparison, is one entire layer. The crucial difference between the two can be seen from above: even though it is not as tall as the triangular piece, the layer/inventory is a complete circle.

An inventory will give your museum what it has never yet accomplished: a complete record of the entire collection at a defined point in time. True, it will not be a very detailed record, but there will be lots of time to add detail later (by adding frosting, putting another layer on top of the first one, and so on). Humans need closure, and so do collections management projects. At the end of an inventory, you will know for certain what you have, because you will have touched, recorded, and photographed every artifact in the collection. To do an inventory, you will need some way of identifying all of the places where your collection is stored. This can be a row/bay/shelf listing, or an area of a room, or some other system. What matters is that someone with a diagram can find the particular location of an object. Next, you need a hard-copy listing of all of the artifacts in the collection – at least according to the collections database and any other records you might have. Finally, you need a way to take photographs as you go. These are record photos, not beauty shots, so a cellphone camera is just fine.

For each artifact, locate its accession number and write it on either a piece of paper or, better yet, a small dry-erase board. Place the written number in front of the artifact and photograph it against a neutral background or on the shelf if it cannot be moved. What matters is getting a reasonably clear photo of the item in which the accession number is visible. On a hard-copy sheet with sequential page numbers (1 of **, 2 of **, and so on, note the storage location, the accession number as it is written on the artifact, and the simplest possible description of the item. If the artifact doesn't appear to have a number, give it a sequential number preceded by an X (X1, X2, X3, and so on) and photograph this with the artifact. This will identify it as an item that was found during the inventory.

Using your diagram of storage areas, keep track of where you have been. If you have more than one team working on the inventory, assign them each a separate location and record what they have done on a master diagram. Will this be tedious? Yes. Will it take some time? Yes, but less time than cataloguing. Once this has been completed for every area where artifacts are stored, reconcile the hard-copy inventory sheets with what the database says you have. Will this be tedious? Yes. Will it take some time? Yes, but less time than cataloguing. Be strong, persevere, reward the staff and volunteers who are doing the work, and see it through to the end.

At the conclusion of this inventory the records of your collection can be sorted into three piles. The good pile contains artifacts with collections records. The two problematic piles contain collections records without artifacts and inventoried artifacts without collections records. There will still be a lot of work to do after the inventory to determine if objects have been misnumbered, placed in the wrong location, overlooked in the inventory, or, for whatever reason, have just left the building, but for the first time you have the information that will make this possible: a comprehensive portrait of your entire collection at a single point in time. You have achieved closure and have taken a significant step towards achieving the twin goals of a well-managed collection: physical and intellectual control.

Why Do We Have It?

Now that you know what you have, you can start to think about why you have it. It is quite possible that by the end of the first week of your inventory project you will be experiencing doubts about whether or not you will ever finish and wondering, first silently and then aloud, why the museum acquired all of this stuff. You might even ask, as you look at a wooden box filled with rusty horseshoe nails or a box of crayons, each of which has its own accession number, "What were they thinking?" (remember, these are all real-life examples). You could respond by doing a Google search for "Soren Kierkegaard" or "Jean-Paul Sartre," realizing that you are a museologist but also an existentialist, deciding that the world makes no sense and leaving it at that.

Or you could make some coffee; buy a box of donuts; gather the staff, volunteers, and board members together; and ask them, "So why do we collect anyways?" Even if you are of a perennially sunny disposition and unlikely to be driven to despair by the idea of photographing 30,000 objects in a month and looking at spreadsheets until your eyes hurt, you should still ask because this is one of the most important questions a community museum professional will ever face.

The period from the mid-eighteenth to the end of the twentieth century could be called "The Great Age of Acquisition." During that time a museum's primary purpose was to collect and diffuse knowledge, and therefore the more it collected, the more knowledge it would have to diffuse. This approach built some of the world's great cultural institutions. For community museums, however, it also led to the situation described at the beginning of this chapter.

So Then Why Do We Collect?

1. Because we would not be a museum if we did not.
2. Because we need to have one or more of everything, right?
3. Because if we do not collect this object now, who will?
4. Because it might be used in an exhibit someday.

5. Because if we say "no," the donor will be mad, or sad, or may not send us a Christmas card, or may never talk to us again.
6. Because if we do not collect this object, something bad might happen, even though we do not know what that might be, or when or even if that might happen.

I am fairly certain that you will hear one or more, or perhaps all, of these reasons when you ask your group the question. To help you prepare for this meeting, here are some talking points:

1. Your museum's mission statement or statement of purpose outlines several reasons why it was founded, and collecting is probably only one of them. Even if you stopped collecting tomorrow, you would not be short of stuff to work with (that is what got you to where you are now, remember?).
2. You are running a cultural institution, not a humane society. Nor are you loading an ark. The renaissance is over, and we all understand that the encyclopedic collection is a myth.
3. Perhaps no one will collect as they might have in the past, and that is not necessarily a problem. Remember, you are running a museum, not a thrift store.
4. You know you can borrow objects from other museums, right?
5. That is a possibility, but there are ways to say "no" that will benefit both you and the donor. See later.
6. Be brave and it will be ok.

For community museums, the liberating, life-changing answer to the question "why do we collect?" is "to tell stories that are important to our community." That, and only that, is the reason. This is one area in which you are allowed to disregard the big picture view and think only of your museum. In fact, it is your job to do so. Once you let go of the idea that your community museum is collecting to save the world or to preserve endangered artifacts, deciding on what should and should not be in your collection becomes refreshingly simple. You are collecting to preserve and share the stories of your community. How do you know what stories are important to your community? Hold on, I will get to that shortly. In the meantime, we are going to think about saying "no." "No" is a pretty strong statement, and it can come across to donors as a rejection of both them and their artifact. "No" is what you say to the person at your door who is trying to sell something you don't want, and it is intended to get them off your porch as quickly as possible.

True, some donors may be approaching you simply to get rid of stuff they no longer want, and for them "thanks, but no" is an appropriate answer. The majority of them, however, will be well-intentioned and are more than likely trying to help. They might think their item is historically or monetarily valuable and would be important to your museum. They might have a story to tell about what the object represents, or it may simply be important to them and so they assume it will be important to the museum as well.

Imagine you are at your desk answering what feels like the tenth letter in the last three months from a donor offering to give the museum their grandmother's wedding dress. Feeling beset, you lean back in your chair and say in an exasperated tone of voice to anyone who will listen, "Why do people keep offering to give us stuff we do not want?" Pause for a moment, count to five, and ask yourself this question: has the museum ever told people what it does want? If not, then donors can be forgiven for showing up with items that it does not. Here are two possible responses to the offer of the wedding dress:

> Dear Mr. and Mrs. Donor: Regarding your offer of Grandma Nellie's wedding dress, I regret to inform you that the museum is unable to accept your proposed donation. Sincerely, The Curator.

> Dear Mr. and Mrs. Donor: Thank you for considering us as a home for Grandma Nellie's wedding dress. I would like to talk with you about its history, but before that I also want to tell you a little bit about the museum and its collections. Our mission statement is "To collect and preserve objects, images and stories that tell the story of the people of Centerville." Since the museum's founding in 1956, we have been acquiring artifacts to fulfill this mission. Now, more than 60 years later, it is safe to say we have largely accomplished that task. We have strong collections of manufactured goods, personal items, images, ephemera, and archival materials to illustrate the history of our community and surrounding towns and villages. What we are most interested in acquiring now are objects specifically related to Centerville. For example, we have a number of wedding dresses in the collection dating from the 1880s to the 1950s. What we are lacking is a wedding dress made by Edna Rogers who for many years operated a women's wear store and dressmaker's shop on Center Street. We know from records in our archives that she clothed many of the town's leading women, but we do not yet have an example of her work in the collection. For more information about what we are collecting now, please see the "What's In Our Collection" page at www.centervillemuseum.org. If you or any of your acquaintances know of an example of Edna's work, we would be most appreciative to hear it. Thank you again for thinking of the museum. Sincerely, The Curator.

One letter stops the correspondence. The other starts a conversation about the museum and its mission and invites participation and further discussion. Notice also the reference to online information. FAQs, summaries of what is in the collection, and a statement about areas in which the museum is actively collecting are valuable additions to your website. If you let your audience know what objects the museum is interested in collecting and explained it well, the conversation with prospective donors will have begun even before they contact you.

If you always say "yes" to proposed donations because you are afraid of the consequences of saying "no," the museum will end up with the collection it deserves. If you are able to make the donation proposal the start of a conversation about what the museum is, what stories it is trying to tell, and what artifacts it needs to tell those stories, you are much more likely to end up with the collection you want and need. The world will not end if you say "no," but (at least in terms of the sustainability of your museum), it might well end if you do not because the costs of storing and managing those collections could take over the budget.

What Should We Do With It?

Now you know what you have, what you are supposed to have, and what you do not have. You have asked important questions of your staff, board members, and volunteers, and you have told the public about what you are collecting and why. These actions will set you up for future success with your collection, but they do not address what to do with the surfeit of objects that the museum already owns. For that you need deaccession. Deaccessioning is a topic in its own right, but it is sufficient here to note that it is a necessary activity for institutions that actively manage their collections.

Normally deaccessioning is a reductive process that makes your collection smaller. This is accomplished by deciding which objects to remove from the collection through the application of predetermined criteria outlined in your bylaws and collections policy. It is not unlike voting someone off the island on an episode of *Survivor*. One by one, the artifacts leave the collection. I would like to offer a different route to the same destination.

Here is a thought experiment that can put your new understanding of the collection, and the reasons why you collect, to good use. Instead of making your collection smaller, try making it larger. Instead of deaccessioning, try thinking about "reaccessioning." One by one, review artifacts or groups of artifacts against what you have decided are the stories your museum needs to tell. It is just like the question often asked at the end of a job reference call: "Knowing what you do now, would you hire this person again?" For a museum artifact, you will ask, "Knowing what we now know about the purpose(s) for which we are collecting, if we did not already own this artifact would we decide to acquire it now?" This is a positive approach, and it allows you to act as a collections committee that is asking the questions it should have asked the first time around. To do this we still need to determine what stories your museum should be telling, and for that we must turn to two key documents that you should have if you do not already: an interpretive plan and a collections plan.

Where Do We Go From Here?

Chances are your institutional mission statement is a general document that broadly defines a goal without providing specifics ("To collect and preserve objects, images, and stories that tell the story of the people of Centerville."). It will likely not change during the life of the institution. While it provides a foundation for the activities the museum will undertake, it does not offer any specific guidance to staff. What you need is some direction that is more specific than the mission statement but broader in scope than the details of day-to-day activities. What you need, in other words, is an interpretive plan and a collections plan.

Unlike the mission statement, these documents can and should be reviewed and updated every few years. They serve as instructions to staff about how to put the mission into practice. While they are supported by policies, which are set by the board, they are developed and implemented by staff. Simply put, an interpretive plan is a strategic plan for the stories your museum will tell. It presents the broad themes that are relevant to the museum's mission. In so doing, it also outlines the scope of the museum's programming and can be used to identify themes that are not relevant to the mission.

An interpretive plan and a collections plan are notionally of equal importance, but for a museum that is focused on visitor engagement, and for whom the visitor experience is the most important outcome, the interpretive plan should guide the development of the collections plan. Remember, you are not trying to save the world. The museum's job is to preserve and share the community's stories. For a reaccessioning project, the most important question you ask of each artifact will be the same one that should have been asked at the collections committee meeting during which it was originally proposed for acquisition: how will this object help us tell our stories? As nice, or beautiful, or rare as it may be, something that does not do that should not be added to your collection. If it is already in your collection, it should go.

A Curator's Reflections on Collections and Collecting

It can be difficult to be objective about a museum collection, particularly if it is one you have had a hand in building. Chances are, if you work as a curator, it was a strong interest in the objects themselves that brought you into museum work in the first place. For you, it is the stuff that matters. As hard as it is to achieve, this objective point of view is what is most required. Passion has its place, but if your task is to make sense of your community museum collection, it is not the most productive place to start. You may not be the only one around your museum with this point of view either. I worked for several years with a collections committee of which I as curator was notionally the chair. The committee comprised mainly board members, most of whom were also collectors of the same kind of material that composed most of the museum's collection. That might seem a good fit – after all, who knows more about collecting than collectors?

In fact, for the same reason, it is the worst possible membership for a collections committee because collectors cannot stop being collectors. As members of the committee, their job is to help the museum build the collection it needs to accomplish its mission. In their private lives, however, their job is to build the collection they want. The two interests do not necessarily align. This became clear for me when at one protracted committee meeting where we were discussing a proposed donation, one member, who was himself a collector, said in mild exasperation, "Hell, John. Why don't you just take them all (the proposed donations). You can

Making Sense of Your Community Museum 21

always sell them afterwards!" It was at that moment the project to develop the museum's first-ever collections plan was born.

As I noted at the beginning of the chapter, an uncontrolled and unexamined collection is of little use to the museum, staff, or public. In this condition, it is more of a liability than an asset and in extreme situations can cause the institution to collapse. I hope that by now it is clear that a few simple questions can help you make sense of your collection and help your collection make sense for your institution.

Suggested references to help you make sense of your community museum collection include the following:

- Elizabeth Wood, Rainey Tisdale, and Trevor Jones (Editors) *Active Collections* (2017) and their website at www.activecollections.org/.
- National Association for Interpretation. *Standards and Practices for Interpretive Planning* (2009).
- James B. Gardner and Elizabeth E. Merritt. *The AAM Guide to Collections Planning* (2004).

2 Collecting Our Culture
Eeyou Cree Collecting at Aanischaaukamikw Cree Cultural Institute

Aanischaaukamikw Cree Cultural Institute

The phrase "decolonize the museum" is now in widespread use in the greater museum field. It refers to analyzing and changing how and why museums, especially long-standing institutions, reflect attitudes that are largely Eurocentric in character. The creation and corrective quality of the movement seek to change what many consider embedded prejudices about why a particular museum exists and how it operates. The outcomes may focus on an entity's public persona but cut to the core of mission implementation.

As an issue, decolonizing is especially voiced about certain museum collections. The focus is on things commonly called ethnographic, archeological, or native by largely white North American or European museum practitioners. These terms are being rejected or redefined as people outside these realms who represent those originally associated with such collections. These communities demand a voice in the ownership, use, and location of the collections under examination. Museums are slowly accepting the change in the collection profiles. This can cause removal of things from existing repositories, new ways of interpreting them, and even their physical alterations. This is a movement that is just beginning and will grow enormously. While much attention has focused on existing museums, new museums are being formed that are owned and operated by members of the communities originally associated with the collections under discussion. This chapter is a superb example of how decolonizing is being implemented in northeastern Canada for the original inhabitants of this region before largely English and French immigrant empires colonized it.

This chapter explains how the Aanischaaukamikw Cree Cultural Institute (ACCI) has been developed and continues to work to strengthen Indigenous Eeyou cultural heritage, including acquisitions processes. Centering Eeyou ways of working and activating a decolonized museological environment demonstrate how the European museological inheritance has been adjusted to meet the needs of this dynamic cultural center. ACCI cares for the culture of the region of Eeyou Istchee, a self-governing region in what is now known as Quebec, Canada. The chapter includes detailed explanations of acquisition processes for permanent collections and loan collections, procedural details relating to acquisitions, and specific methodological examples that reveal how the work enacts Eeyou worldviews

DOI: 10.4324/9781003216384-3

Collecting Our Culture 23

and ways of being. It is written without a single voice or single authorship – this contribution was collaboratively written by ACCI.

Introduction to Aanischaaukamikw

Aanischaaukamikw Cree[1] Cultural Institute opened in 2011 after decades of planning by Eeyou Elders and community members. Located in Ouje-Bougoumou, ACCI is the regional cultural institute for Eeyou Istchee, a self-governing region in what is now known as Quebec that has ten Eeyou communities: Whapmagoostui (Great Whale), Chisasibi (Fort George), Eastmain, Wemindji (Paint Hills), Waskaganish (Rupert's House), Nemaska, Waswanipi, Ouje-Bougoumou, Mistissini, and Washaw Sibi[2] (Figures 2.1 and 2.2). Activities related to the institute include educational programming related to Eeyou culture, management of a cultural archive, library, museum collection, and a permanent exhibition. The following mandate explains its mission, which is imbued with Eeyou values:

> Aanischaaukamikw flows from the knowledge that Cree culture must be captured, maintained, shared, celebrated, and practiced . . . it is a living, breathing symbol of our determination to preserve and share the stories and legends, the music, the pictures, and the physical objects that show our unique interaction with the land, expressed through hunting, fishing, trapping, and underscored with a reverence for the land we have walked since time immemorial.[3]

Acquisitions at Aanischaaukamikw

Collecting for Aanischaaukamikw started many decades before the institute opened. In 2011 there was a small acquisitions backlog in the library, archives, and museum collections. By 2014 the backlog of processing was mostly complete, and the policies related to acquisitions and collections management could be refined to better suit the ongoing programming and strategic goals. The acquisitions policy was revised in 2014, with accompanying procedures drafted in 2015 that are continuously updated as needs arise. This chapter will focus on the museum collecting, but our archives and library collections have expanded rapidly in the first ten years of the institute being open.

Acquisitions Policy and Governance

Our acquisition policy lays out the guidelines for what we collect, which focuses on material and intangible expressions of Eeyou culture that enable us to undertake activities related to our mandate.

Our general "collecting plan" is defined in our acquisitions policy:

> Through its collections, ACCI documents and presents the history and contemporary contribution of Eeyou Istchee culture and customs. ACCI is

24 *Aanischaaukamikw Cree*

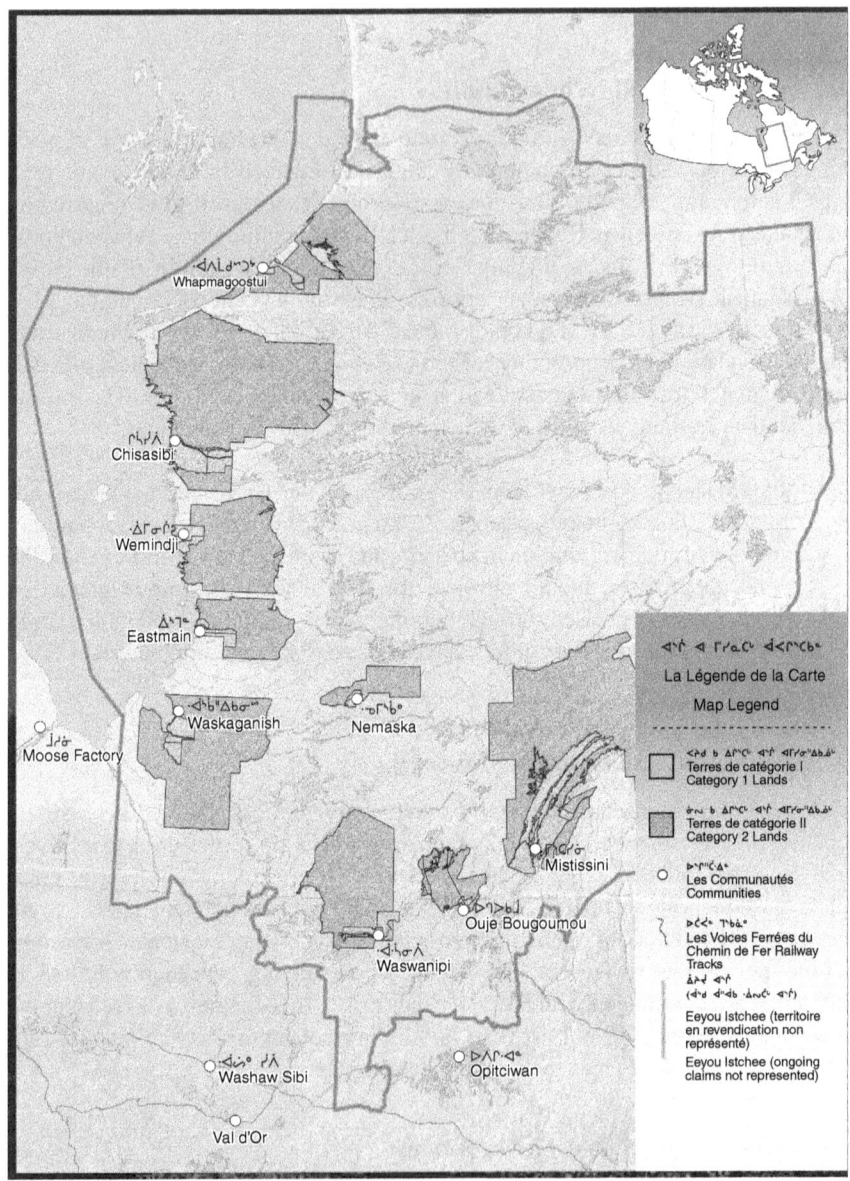

Figure 2.1 Map of Eeyou Istchee

committed to the acquisitions of collections that are unique, and a direct reflection of its interests. The collections are formed through a considered and deliberate identification of two and three dimensional artefacts, objects, media, ephemera, archival material and representations of intangible

Figure 2.2 Aanischaaukamikw Cree Cultural Institute (Photograph: Mitch Linet, 2012)

material that best reflects the history, customs and culture of Eeyou Istchee. The collections strengths and weaknesses must be evaluated by ACCI on a regular basis to ensure that growth is proceeding within the defined parameters, and that ACCI is deriving the maximum benefit from the resources available to it.[4]

Our policy also includes acquisition information organized under these headings: Roles and Responsibilities Relating to Acquisitions; Scope of the ACCI Collections (Library, Archive, Museum); Acquisitions Criteria by Collection; Common Acquisitions Criteria; Methods of Acquisition; Restricted Acquisitions; Documentation of Acquisitions; and Resolution of Questionable Acquisitions). Acquisitions are administered by our collections registrar, who chairs the Acquisitions Committee.

The Acquisitions Committee is composed of our executive director, the director of programs, the coordinator of collections and exhibitions, and the conservator. When the acquisition is for the museum collection, the curator will be included. When the acquisition is for the accessioned library collection, the librarian is included. Only the Rare Books and Special Collections go through the formal accessioning process in the library. When the acquisition is a new archival collection, the archivist is included. The registrar gathers all of the necessary details about a proposed acquisition and circulates it to the Acquisitions Committee by email (Figure 2.3). Usually by the time the email is circulated we have discussed internally any of the possible challenges with the acquisition, so the approval or rejection is usually just a formalization of all of the information about the

26 Aanischaaukamikw Cree

Source	▓▓▓▓▓
Date of deposit (if applicable)	As soon as approved by acquisitions committee
Proposed method of acquisition	Donation
Significance of Object	▓▓▓▓▓ lived in Eeyou Istchee for a many years. ▓▓ taught in Moosonee from August 1958 to June 1959. Eastmain from September 1962 to June 1969 and in Fort George from Fall of 1972 to Spring of 1973. ▓▓▓ recently passed away in May, 2015 and her friends ▓▓▓▓ with her co-executor are looking to donate photos that ▓▓ had taken during her time in Eeyou Istchee (still need to be sorted out by ▓▓▓), a copy of her journals, 2 baby rattles (no photos yet, similar to one ones on ACCI web page) and the beaded bag to ACCI. My thoughts are that the beaded bag may be from Moosonee?
Acquisitions Policy Criteria for Artifacts to be accepted into: Core collection (objects) & Eeyou Istchee Fonds (Photos)	Historical or contemporary artifacts acquired by people who lived or worked in Cree territory
Brief Condition Statement	Good condition
Associated Costs	**Curatorial Costs** 2 Small trays: 6$ 1 Large tray: 7$ Storage costs: 10$/year Label printing: 12$ **Transportation costs** +/- 80$ shipping with Post Canada **Digitization** Digital Storage: $30 per year per GB Digital Upkeep: $0.50 per year per GB
Photograph(s)	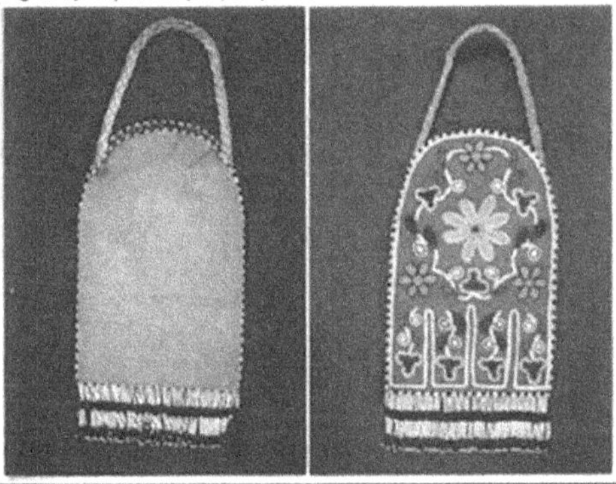
ACQUISITIONS COMMITTEE – APPROVE / REJECT / DEFER	
▓▓▓▓ [Executive Director]	
▓▓▓▓ [Interim Director of Programs]	
▓▓▓▓ [Co-ordinator of Collections and Exhibits]	
▓▓▓▓ [Conservator]	
▓▓▓▓ [Collections Officer]	Approve

Figure 2.3 Example Acquisitions Proposal Email

acquisition to document the final decision. We endeavor to have acquisitions approved before they arrive on site to avoid having to dispose of items that do not meet our collecting scope (more on this later).

Once a year we report to our board of directors with a summary of all of the acquisitions that have come in since the last meeting. When ACCI first opened, the policy stated that the board of directors had to approve all acquisitions.

Collecting Our Culture 27

This was found to be unworkable in practice because the delay in formal acceptance meant that cataloguing and assigning object numbers could not be finalized without the board approval. We revised the policy and procedures to work better for our institution and to make the best use of the board's time for higher-level decisions.

Museum Collection Acquisitions Procedures

We have written procedures that are updated as needed, but we also try to be flexible and accommodating to make sure we meet the needs of the Eeyou communities. Our collections have come in from a variety of sources. For example, the Cree Nation Government had a campaign to collect cultural belongings in the 1990s, resulting in what we call the Cree Regional Authority collection, which was the name of the regional branch of the Cree Nation Government based in Nemaska (2012.09) for many years (Figure 2.4). This collection was stored in the regional office as it was gathered and donated to ACCI upon opening in 2011. Unfortunately over the years in storage, many of the items in this collection had lost information about the community and maker's name, but we have been able to identify some of these details from people and family members recognizing the patterns and designs made by relatives. This is an important point for all museums with Indigenous belongings in their collections – people and communities will often recognize the designs made by relatives. Many patterns are passed down over the years and are still in use in families today.

Figure 2.4 Some Examples From the CRA Nemaska Collection

Eeyou community members have been incredibly supportive of our institute. Since 2011, we have received donations (composed of single and multiple items) from ten Eeyou entities and 36 Eeyou community members (Figure 2.5). We have purchased collections from Eeyou community members on 36 occasions and twice from Eeyou entities. We have received 29 donations from non-Eeyou individuals and three from non-Eeyou entities. We have purchased 11 collections from non-Eeyou entities or individuals and commissioned Eeyou crafts or artwork 17 times. We have received transfers from other museums on four occasions.

Non-Eeyou people who worked in our region have been the source of donations to our museum collections and also to our library and archives. Some examples of well-known anthropologists who worked in our region in the twentieth century and who have made donations of their research collections or archives include Harvey Feit, Richard Preston, Pierrette (Paula) Desy, Cath Oberholtzer, Adrian Tanner, and Marguerite Mackenzie. We are researching other students and professionals who worked in our region and hope to increase the amount of material that is returned to us.

In the early years of opening, we made some purchases to supplement the historical collections, though these come with very little provenance information. Generally there is a stylistic guess as to the general region these belongings were extracted from, with a general date span, and we have not been able to identify the maker or community for any of these, but we are always hopeful this will be discovered in future research by our communities. More often than not, these collections tend to be linked in some way to the fur trade, which brought large numbers of Europeans into our region for the purposes of

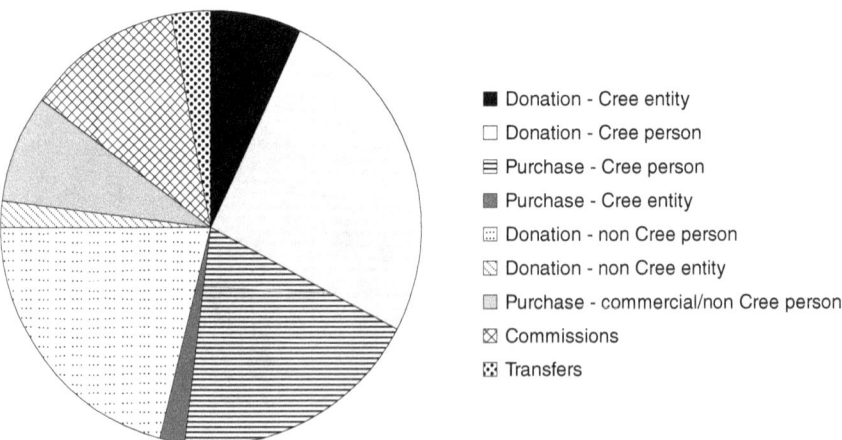

Figure 2.5 Graphic of Acquisitions by Method and Source Type 2011–2020

exploiting our resources for personal and corporate gain. These days we tend to opt not to pay for our own culture or extracted belongings, and we hope that not participating in commercial sales of our historical belongings will mean the capitalist market value is reduced in favor of valuing the return of these ancestral belongings to our home region.

As of 2020 we do have one formal repatriation request that is pending with Ville de Montreal. This is for a ceremonial beaded hood that has been linked to the Gunner family of Mistissini,[5] whose living relatives wish for the hood to be returned permanently to the region via Aanischaaukamikw. We had the hood on loan for one year, but now we are in the process of requesting to have it back permanently. Under the many centuries of colonialism in our region, we are certain many of these belongings were not giving up willingly by their owners. It is more likely our possessions were taken under duress; in exchange for food when we faced starvation because of overhunting by outsiders; for payment of debts encouraged by traders[6]; under the pressure of missionaries who were teaching us to disregard our beliefs in favor of theirs; or even stolen from graves and our seasonal camps when we were hunting elsewhere.

In the coming years we will likely seek additional transfers of sacred and ceremonial belongings that are currently incarcerated in museums in Canada, North America, and Europe, especially England. We have plans underway to expand our storage capabilities so we can accommodate a large-scale return of our belongings as museums recognize that our belongings need to be in our region. We understand that very few of these belongings will have the documentation that enables us to say for certain they are from Eeyou Istchee, but our people traveled widely in the region, and if any location is recorded, it tends to be where the final transaction took place, rather than where something was made. We will likely seek regional transfers for these belongings so we can share them with our close neighbors, the Innu/Montagnais and the Naskapi nations,[7] in ways that reflect our worldviews rather than imported capitalist notions of individual ownership.

Our acquisitions procedures and policy prefer that we accept only materials that are from our region. We have had to deal with a few collections that were clearly not from our region, but that ended up on site for a variety of reasons. These collections will be circulated to the Acquisitions Committee, but they are usually rejected unless there is a compelling link to the region. When the proposals are rejected, we find alternative repositories for the collections. There have been two recent instances of rehoming collections. We received a donation of a collection of baskets that we identified as being from the east of us, in Mi'kmaq territory. We contacted the K'Taqmkuk Mi'kmaq Historical Museum[8] and they agreed to accept them. Another example was when the regional airline, Air Creebec, sent us a large glass mounted photograph of their founder, Billy Diamond. We already have a framed copy of this photograph in our gathering and performance space, which is named after him ("the Billy Diamond Hall") and features a mural by Virginia Bordeleau of his lifetime achievements entitled "Hommage au chef Billy Diamond."

We contacted his home nation, Waskaganish Cree Nation, and they were happy to receive the glass mounted photograph to display in their band offices.

Special Considerations and Activating UNDRIP

Compared to museums that gather encyclopedic collections of "other," our focus on *our own* Eeyouch history and culture, and our unique location within a region of Eeyouch experts on these topics means we have developed additional ways of working with acquisitions that may challenge museology that still centers on European foundations. This section will outline some of the special considerations we have in place related to acquiring different types of collections.

Many of these special considerations demonstrate how we have activated the requirements put forth in the articles of the United Nations Declaration on the Rights of Indigenous Peoples (UNDRIP).[9] We encourage all museums to work in spirit of these articles even if their country has not yet ratified the declaration. The most relevant articles for our purposes are:

Article 11.1: "Indigenous peoples have the right to practice and revitalize their cultural traditions and customs. This includes the right to maintain, protect and develop the past, present and future manifestations of their cultures, such as archaeological and historical sites, artefacts, designs, ceremonies, technologies and visual and performing arts and literature."

Article 11.2: "States [nation states/countries] shall provide redress through effective mechanisms, which may include restitution, developed in conjunction with Indigenous peoples, with respect to their cultural, intellectual, religious and spiritual property taken without their free, prior and informed consent or in violation of their laws, traditions and customs."

Article 12.1: "Indigenous peoples have the right to manifest, practise, develop and teach their spiritual and religious traditions, customs and ceremonies; the right to maintain, protect, and have access in privacy to their religious and cultural sites; the right to the use and control of their ceremonial objects; and the right to the repatriation of their human remains."

Article 12.2: "States shall seek to enable the access and/or repatriation of ceremonial objects and human remains in their possession through fair, transparent and effective mechanisms developed in conjunction with indigenous peoples concerned."

Article 13.1: "Indigenous peoples have the right to revitalize, use, develop and transmit to future generations their histories, languages, oral traditions, philosophies, writing systems and literatures, and to designate and retain their own names for communities, places and persons."

Article 15.1: "Indigenous peoples have the right to the dignity and diversity of their cultures, traditions, histories and aspirations which shall be appropriately reflected in education and public information."

Article 15.2: "States shall take effective measures, in consultation and cooperation with the Indigenous peoples concerned, to combat prejudice and eliminate discrimination and to promote tolerance, understanding and good relations among Indigenous peoples and all other segments of society."

Core and Living Collections

Our permanent collection is divided into Core and Living collections. Only the Core collection is accessioned, though both collections are catalogued and follow the same acquisition process. This was purposefully done so that we can use the Living collection as a handling collection for active learning and for interactive exhibits. Our acquisitions policy explains the difference in these two collections, and the collection allocation is determined during the acquisition approval process.

> The Core Collection is the permanent collection and consists of objects of intrinsic value that document the mission statement of the museum. The objects allocated to this category are considered valuable and irreplaceable. Preservation is of utmost priority in any decision regarding the care and use of this collection. The objects are catalogued and accessioned. The objects in the Core Collection are recognized for their age, rarity, potentially fragile condition, and are subject to the highest level of security.[10]
>
> The Living Collection consists of non-accessioned objects of any form used for display or educational purposes. Their period of use in ACCI can be temporary, depending on their intended use, or they can be physically installed within ACCI. The Living Collection may contain duplicates or replica objects that can be handled and/or circulated for educational purposes without the conservation or security constraints required by objects in the Core Collection . . . The Living Collection objects are catalogued for tracking purposes and to retain their contextual information. Exhibit props will not necessarily be added to the Living Collection but will be maintained on a separate basic inventory list.[11]

Sometimes we will acquire a collection that is split between Core and Living collections. For example, in 2016 we received funding from the Cree Nation Government for a project that commissioned Elders from each community to make beaded or embroidered saasinh (vamps) or astis saasin (glove or mitten vamp)[12] (Figure 2.6). We asked the Elders to make a matching pair, and we have split these so one piece will go into the Core collection and one piece will go into the Living collection. We intend to display these together, in our "Featured Object" case, which is in the entrance area of our building. After that, we intend to keep the items designated for the Core collection in our secure collections storage area and display the items designated for the Living collection in our permanent exhibit as a sensory experience for visitors. Our exhibit has many examples of embroidery and beadwork, but these are contained within display cases. Adding these outside of the cases means our visitors can touch the beadwork and the embroidery and smell the scent of smoked

32 *Aanischaaukamikw Cree*

moose hide. We also wanted to add these as tactile opportunities for visually impaired visitors.

Community Loans

Since 2014 we have expanded our community loans programs and drafted our current loans policy to take specific needs of our community members into consideration.[13] This means we work beyond standard museum loan principles. For

Figure 2.6 Elders' Project Examples

example, we will accept loans from community members for safe-keeping and storage of their belongings, including any sacred or ceremonial collections that require specific protocols. Other ceremonial belongings may be lent with instructions that only a family member of the lender can handle the belonging directly because the belonging is imbued with a special protective relationship built between the owner and the belonging. This was the case with a makaahiikan[14] (Figure 2.7) lent as part of a child's first snowshoe walk ceremonial outfit.

We accept loans even if they are not to be displayed. We will accommodate short-term returns of loaned belongings if the family needs them back for a few days to use in a new ceremony (Figure 2.8). We accept loans from Cree entities that need a secure storage space. Some of our largest loaned collections are from other Eeyou entities: from Eenou Corporation, we have a selection of their Indigenous artwork collection; from Cree Native Arts & Crafts Association, we have a selection of crafts made in the region; and from the Cree Nation Government, we have a collection of Indigenous artwork that was commissioned for the 1990s exhibition "Weejeethoon: African Life Through the Eyes of Canadian Indigenous Peoples." Most of the art in these loans are by artists from Indigenous nations outside of Eeyou Istchee, but we have accepted them on loan so we can promote and care for these spectacular collections.

Figure 2.7 First Snowshoe Walk Ceremony

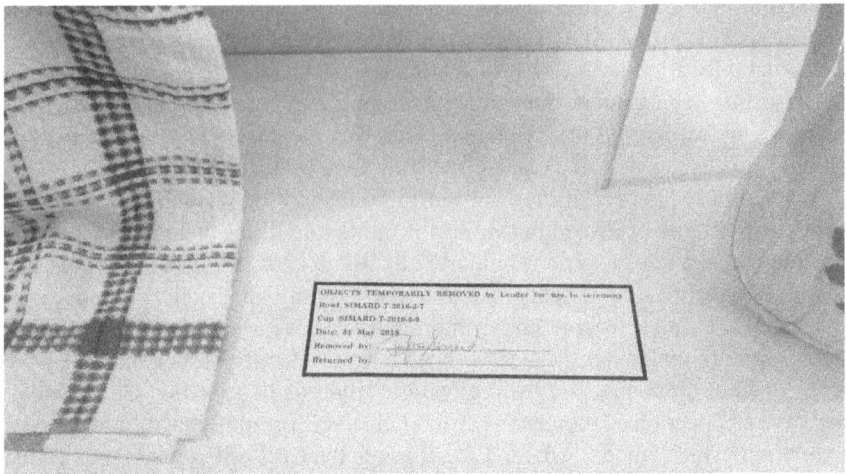

Figure 2.8 Loan Withdrawn for Ceremony

Photographs and Media Acquisitions

We have an expanding collection of photographs taken in Eeyou Istchee. These are part of our archive collection, where we have a fonds called Eeyou Istchee Media Collection (EIMC). We are thinking beyond standard archival principles where the "creator" of material is centered through the naming convention and other descriptive standards. We chose to center the region, and communities, so the material is easy to find and to ensure our way of organizing our archival collections meets the needs of the community members in ways that make sense to them. We do have some archival collections named after the "creator," but these are larger collections, and many of them were arranged in the early days of opening before we had thought through how we can apply decolonizing principles.

In our EIMC fonds we collect photographs and other media (audio, video) that is anticipated to be a single donation of media only (not paper/documentary type archives). Despite formally having copyright transferred with most of these collections, we also work *beyond copyright* to seek permission of the people shown in each photograph (or their living relatives if they have passed) if we desire to use them for any public reason, for example, exhibitions or publications. This is particularly important for photographs and other media gathered in the predigital age, because any consents from that period need to be reconfirmed for the multitude of new ways of using these materials.

Digital Reference Materials

Many collections of material about our region are cared for by institutions outside of our region, especially in urban areas like Montreal, Ottawa, and Gatineau. Two

Cree youth worked on researching what archives are in different places as summer students funded by Young Canada Works and a Cree youth program in 2018. Whenever possible, they made or requested digital copies of entire collections for us to have as reference copies. When this material is archival in nature, we have chosen to keep them as archives so we can control access to them and maintain the integrity required by the holder of the original material. In most cases we have added these data sets to the Eeyou Istchee Media Collection, and instead of a transfer of title document, we have a license agreement that details the ways we are permitted to use these collections. This agreement makes clear that any uses not specified there will be referred to the institution holding the collection. Our main goal is expanding our digital resources so that we have a central repository of all cultural archives relating to our region – whether or not we have the originals of papers and photographs is not as important to us as having access for our community members. We have limited storage space, so accepting copies of collections that are already digitized means we only need server space for these and not space for more boxes.

Case Study of an Acquisition

Instead of speaking in detail about one acquisition story, we will share a group of recent acquisitions that are related to a project that commenced in 2017, "Rediscovering the Tradition of Painted Caribou Coats in Eeyou Istchee," funded by the Arts Council of Canada's Indigenous funding stream "Creating, Knowing and Sharing."[15] This multiyear project focused on putting community-based research and contemporary knowledge into conversation with our ancestors' belongings to generate new information and creative outputs inspired by this research. Some of the project activities included funding artists-in-residence, organizing trips to take Elders to see belongings that are now in museums, and art workshops in communities. We have been holistic in approach and acquired caribou hides directly from the people who hunted and butchered the caribou; re-creations of bone and antler tools carved by a master carver from animals he hunted; and artwork from Eeyou artists that was inspired by nature, as our ancestors were inspired by nature for the decorations they painted on their coats. All of these acquisitions relate in some way to the research relating to these caribou coats and the matching accessories that were worn by our ancestors (Figure 2.9).

Painted caribou coats are examples of what our historical belongings can inspire in the minds of our community members as we renew our traditions using intergenerational knowledge transmissions. The components of the historical coats are interesting to our local scientists because of the ways the materials have been sourced and used in the creation of the coats, from the organics used in the paint to the methods of applying the design with bone and antler tools. The regional tradition of the caribou hunt is currently being affected by climate change, and the coat can be used as a discussion point to remember the caribou hunts of the past and changes that have happened over time. These coats have enormous contemporary research value for our communities, the region, and the nation.

36 *Aanischaaukamikw Cree*

Figure 2.9 Acquisitions From Our Painted Caribou Coats Research Project

The acquisitions described here came to us from different people and by different acquisition methods, some of which stretch typical definitions and might even end up requiring new terminologies. The common theme between these acquisitions is their relation to the painted coats research project and that they demonstrate our strength and resilience in the face of recent colonial genocide attempts[16] and are evidence of the continuity between our contemporary Eeyou community members and the ways of our ancestors, since time immemorial.

Prepared Caribou Hide (2019.15.1)

We acquired some caribou hides that had been fixed white, which means the hide is not smoke tanned, only brain tanned and left to dry. Caribou are decreasing in the region, and there are calls to limit or ban hunting so they have an opportunity to regenerate their herd sizes. With this in mind, we appreciated the potential rarity of these complete hides and added this one to the Core collection at Aanischaaukamikw so that we can preserve it in its entirety going forward. This hide was prepared by Tina George of Whapmagoostui in winter 2018, and we acquired it from her by purchase.

Antler Bone and Painting Tools (2019.16.01-.08)

Gordon Shecapio Blacksmith is a member of Ouje-Bougoumou Cree Nation and is well known as a carver of wood, bone, and antler. Using the photographs of the tools currently on loan to us from the Royal Ontario Museum, Gordon created a set of painting tools for our research team to experiment with. We acquired these from him as a commission, which for our purposes means we asked him to make us something specific, following existing examples. We split these between the Core and Living collections.

Painted Hide Samplers (2019.17.01-.02)

Natasia Mukash of Whapmagoostui Cree Nation, the only fly-in community in Eeyou Istchee, was one of the project researchers and is a well-known visual artist, curator, crafts woman, and owner of Painted Stone Studio.[17] Natasia experimented with applying paint to hide using the bone and antler tools made by Gordon. She used one piece of caribou hide and one piece of commercially tanned moose hide and sent them to us to add to the project archive. Because they are displayable and go well with the tools we commissioned from Gordon, we opted to use our acquisition processes to add them to the Living collection as a donation[18] in case they are ever needed for workshop demonstrations.

Artwork by Natasia Mukash (2020.05.01-.02)

Natasia has often painted or created artwork that depicts or is inspired by caribou, especially in the months when the regional herd transits through her home community of Whapmagoostui. In 2019 Natasia painted a series called "Caribou Universe," which included these two paintings, *Past/Future* and *Reflection*. We acquired these by purchase for our Core collection.

Artwork by Tim Whiskeychan (2019.02.01-.04; 2019.03.01-.86)

Tim Whiskeychan is a well-known artist from Waskaganish Cree Nation. Tim completed an artist-in-residency with art workshops at Aanischaaukamikw in November 2018 on the theme of "Inspirations from Nature – How the Land Can Inspire Artists." During these workshops Tim demonstrated his innovative technique of placing a piece of paper over a crushed aluminum pop can, rubbing the surface with charcoal, and then creating art from whatever he sees within the resulting design. Our standard artist-in-residency contract requests that artwork created during the residency is offered to us for purchase first, so we purchased three of the artworks made during the residency and Tim donated one to us. These were all added to our Core collection. Tim donated 86 of the pop can charcoal rubbings to us. These have been added to our Core collection.

Artwork by Margaret Orr (2019.13.01 ab; 2019.13.02)

Margaret Orr is a well-known multimedia artist and curator from Chisasibi Cree Nation and was one of the project researchers. Margaret recently completed her MFA at the University of Saskatchewan in Regina, and her graduating exhibition, titled *10,000 Drowned*, was about the 10,000 caribou who drowned when Hydro Quebec opened the spill gate at the Caniapiscau Reservoir in Eeyou Istchee.[19]

Margaret completed an artist-in-residency at Aanischaaukamikw in October 2019, where she created these three art pieces. We acquired these from her by purchase for our Core collection.

Contemporary Creations by Margaret Orr (2020.06.01-.02ab)

From January to March 2020 Margaret traveled to a selection of Eeyou communities to lead workshops where community members could make creations based on the teachings she had learned from the painted caribou coats project. She needed to make some examples to show to the participants to inspire them with creative possibilities. These days hide belongings are usually decorated with beadwork or embroidery, which can be time consuming and difficult to master. Margaret shared that participants were excited to paint decorations, which opened this artistic mode of expression to everyone, especially when they learned that painting was also done by our ancestors on their belongings.

Margaret created an Aspichinaakin (gun case)[20] out of canvas (2020.06.01) and painted it with contemporary interpretations inspired by our ancestors' designs on their caribou hide belongings. She spent time mixing paints so the colors were similar to the natural paints and pigments used on the coats, which were originally made from natural sources found on the land like ochre, tree bark, and fish eggs. The whiteness of the canvas gives an idea of what the painted coats would have looked like when they were freshly painted, with vibrant colors and designs that carried the stories of the original wearer. Margaret donated[21] the gun case to Aanischaaukamikw after the workshops were finished, and we have added it to our Core collection.

Margaret also created a pair of child-sized mittens (2020.06.02ab) that she painted with designs inspired by personal reflections. The mittens are painted on smoke-tanned moose hide rather than caribou hide. Margaret made these during workshops that took place while she was working on site at Aanischaaukamikw. The workshops were hosted by Aanischaaukamikw, Cree Native Arts & Crafts Association, and the Ouje-Bougoumou Justice Department each evening for four nights in the entrance area of our building. Margaret donated[22] the mittens to Aanischaaukamikw, and they are now in our Core collection.

Painted Caribou Hide by Margaret Orr, Paula Menarick, Cree-Lynn Shecapio, and Emily Sam (2020.07.01)

In August 2019 during research workshops for the painted caribou coats project at Aanischaaukamikw, Paula Menarick, Cree-Lynn Shecapio, Emily Sam, and Margaret Orr created a contemporary version of a painted caribou hide inspired by historical examples of painted hides that are now in museums.[23] Paula and Margaret were the workshop leaders. Cree-Lynn was a youth participant, and Emily was a workshop attendee as a knowledge keeper. Paula and Emily are from Chisasibi Cree Nation, though Paula now lives near Ouje-Bougoumou and has very close connections to the community there. They used contemporary inspirations and traditional teachings to decorate a white caribou hide.

We needed it to pass through the formal acquisition process so our registrar could assign the catalogue number because it is being referenced in our publications and reports about the project. This is an unusual instance of artwork being accessioned into our Core collection before it is complete, with the provision that the artists can work on it until they feel it is complete. We will not include any timescale on this "finishing" to reflect that the artwork is a living creation with a spirit connected to, and reflecting, the spirits of the artists.

When doing our acquisitions paperwork, we had to think carefully about whether the method of acquisition would be "donation," as it was for the gun case and the mittens, or "commission," even though we did not specify any parameters for this creation. In the end we opted for "commission" because we had requested that something creative be made at the research workshops using caribou hide that we could add to our collection, we provided all of the materials used, and all of the attendees received a daily honorarium for their participation. We are not entirely sure that "commission" is the correct term, but have used in it in the absence of anything we could find that would fit better.

Conclusion

This chapter outlined the ways that ACCI in Eeyou Istchee has shaped our acquisition processes to reflect our Eeyou way of life. We have been open for almost ten years and have modified what was originally in place in 2011 so that our ways of working are tailored to meet and center on the needs of our Eeyouch community members. We hope that our case study is useful to other Indigenous cultural centers and that it demonstrates to non-Indigenous entities that care for our historical belongings that not only are our communities are thriving, so the original impetus for collecting "disappearing" cultures is well and truly defunct but also how inspirational and important these historical belongings are for our contemporary communities to strengthen the connections to our ancestors in our own way and in our own territories.

Notes

1. Eeyou (pl. Eeyouch) means "the people" in our dialect of Iiyiyiumuwin (the Cree language). "Cree" is a language used across Canada, with many dialects and a descriptive term that Eeyouch refer to themselves by, though our name for ourselves is Eeyou in the coastal area and Eenou in the inland communities. Eeyou Istchee means "the people of the land" and refers to our self-governing territory that spans 5,271 km² (2,035 sq mi), though our original territory prior to colonization spanned 450,000 square kilometers (170,000 sq mi): https://en.wikipedia.org/wiki/Eeyou_Istchee_(territory). For this chapter we will use Eeyou and Cree interchangeably but we are only referring to our own area.
2. The building itself has some Cree entities as tenants: the tourism and marketing agency for the region, Cree Outfitting and Tourism Association (COTA), externally marketed as Eeyou Istchee Baie-James: Escape Like Never Before; Cree Native Arts & Crafts Association (CNACA); and some staff from the Cree Nation Government.
3. http://creeculturalinstitute.ca/about/mission-and-vision/
4. ACCI Collections Acquisition Policy 2.3.1, Section 2.0.
5. For more on this please see www.cbc.ca/news/canada/north/rare-beaded-hood-returns-to-cree-territory-1.3543066; www.cbc.ca/news/canada/north/cree-ask-for-return-of-ceremonial-hood-1.5227416; https://aptnnews.ca/2019/08/02/cree-hood/
6. It's well documented in the archives of the Hudson Bay Company that the post managers encouraged us to accept credit, which we sometimes were not able to pay. See John McLean and John E. Langdon, *Notes of a Twenty-Five Years' Service in the Hudson's Bay Territory*, Vol. 1 & 2, R. Bentley, London, 1849. In 1670 the king of England appropriated thousands of kilometers of land from Indigenous nations in what is known known as Canada and called this territory Rupert's Land. This was done without any consultation with Indigenous nations. This territory was leased to the Hudson's Bay Company for the purposes of extraction of resources, again without consultation or permission from Indigenous nations. In 1869 the Hudson Bay Company *sold* this stolen land to the Dominion of Canada, which had formed in 1867, thus expanding the territory of Canada, and again, without any consultation or remuneration to Indigenous nations who had lived there since time immemorial.
7. For more on the overlap and intersections between the Eeyou/Eenou Cree, the Montagnais/Innu and the Naskapi please see John Bishop and Kevin Brousseau, 'I Speak Cree, not Innu: Ethnically United, Ethnonymically Divided?' in Stephan Gervais, Raffaele Iacovino and Mary Anne Poutanen (eds), *Engaging with Diversity: Multidisciplinary Reflections on Plurality from Quebec*, Diversitas, Tribal Authority, Vol. 23, 2018, pp. 159–183, and Jose Mailhot, 'Beyond Everyone's Horizon Stand the Naskapi', *Ethnohistory*, vol. 33, no. 4, 1986, pp. 384–418.
8. www.sgibnl.ca/ktaqmkuk-mikmaw-cultural-historic-museum-newfoundland/
9. United Nations Human Rights Office of the High Commissioner. *Declaration on the rights of Indigenous Peoples*. Retrieved 1 June 2017 from www.ohchr.org/EN/Issues/IPeoples/Pages/Declaration.aspx
10. ACCI Acquisitions Policy 2.4.1 – Section 4.3.2 Museum Core Collection.
11. ACCI Acquisitions Policy 2.4.1 – Section 4.3.3 Museum Living Collection.

12 For more about this project see Tania Larivière, 'Eeyou-Eenou Artwork Through the Generations', *Air Creebec Inflight Magazine*, Winter 2018, pp. 32–35.
13 Aanischaaukamikw Cree Cultural Institute, 'Beyond Property and Trade: Establishing a Community Loans Program', *MUSE Magazine*, January/February 2019, pp. 14–19.
14 A makaahiikan acts as a walking stick and scoop for snow and ice and guides the owner safely over dangerous terrain. There is no English or French equivalent, so we use the Eeyou word, and on the English and French labels have (snow scoop / shovel) in brackets. This also demonstrates how we center the Cree language in our exhibits.
15 https://canadacouncil.ca/funding/grants/creating-knowing-sharing
16 For example, the residential schools program. www.trc.ca/about-us/trc-findings.html
17 www.facebook.com/natasiamukash/
18 We thought donation as the method was more appropriate than commission here because we did not ask Natasia to create these – it was simply part of her research process, and she used her own materials.
19 This opening of the spill gate released a torrent of water that rushed down the Caniapiscau River, killing 10,000 caribou in the fall of 1984 during their annual fall migration south.
20 In Eeyou Istchee we hunt using rifles and shotguns (and other methods); these are usually carried in a canvas or hide bags that are decorated. We decorate our hunting gear and clothing to honor the animals so they give themselves to us.
21 We had some internal discussion about if this should be a donation or a commission and opted for donation because Margaret was not obliged to give this to us, nor did we request her to make this.
22 We chose to use donation for the same reasons outlined for the gun case.
23 The historical examples are usually either ceremonial robes or decorations for our tipis used at special times of the year.

Bibliography

Published Sources

Aanischaaukamikw Cree Cultural Institute 2019, 'Beyond Property and Trade: Establishing a Community Loans Program', *MUSE Magazine*, January/February, pp. 14–19.

Bishop, J. & Brousseau, K. 2018, 'I Speak Cree, not Innu: Ethnically United, Ethnonymically Divided?' in S. Gervais, R. Iacovino & M. Anne Poutanen (eds.) *Engaging with Diversity: Multidisciplinary Reflections on Plurality from Quebec*, Diversitas, Canada, Vol. 23, pp. 159–183.

Larivière, T. 2018, 'Eeyou-Eenou Artwork Through the Generations', *Air Creebec Inflight Magazine*, Winter, pp. 32–35.

Mailhot, J. 1986, 'Beyond Everyone's Horizon Stand the Naskapi', *Ethnohistory*, vol. 33, no. 4, pp. 384–418.

McLean, J. & Langdon, J.E. 1849, *Notes of a Twenty-Five Years' Service in the Hudson's Bay Territory*, R. Bentley, London, Vol. 1 & 2. Available from: http://archive.org/details/notesoftwentyfiv01mclc.

United Nations Human Rights Office of the High Commissioner, 'Declaration on the rights of Indigenous Peoples'. Available from: www.ohchr.org/EN/Issues/IPeoples/Pages/Declaration.aspx [1 June 2017].

Unpublished Sources

ACCI Collections Acquisition Policy 2.3.1.

Websites

https://en.wikipedia.org/wiki/Eeyou_Istchee_(territory)
http://creeculturalinstitute.ca/about/mission-and-vision/
www.cbc.ca/news/canada/north/rare-beaded-hood-returns-to-cree-territory-1.3543066
www.cbc.ca/news/canada/north/cree-ask-for-return-of-ceremonial-hood-1.5227416
https://aptnnews.ca/2019/08/02/cree-hood/
www.sgibnl.ca/ktaqmkuk-mikmaw-cultural-historic-museum-newfoundland/
https://canadacouncil.ca/funding/grants/creating-knowing-sharing
www.trc.ca/about-us/trc-findings.html

3 Strategies for Acquiring Contemporary Art
Creativity and Collaboration

Jennifer Jankauskas[1]

A major issue facing museums today challenges past practices to almost completely ignore, some might say purposely reject, contemporary art made by non-white, nonmale artists. The reality of these visual absences was true for museums involved with contemporary art regardless of size, budget, location, and mission. Occasionally so-called "outsider art" might be shown that was made by individuals with no formal art school training or customary academic resume. Inevitably the pieces were seen as cute naive curiosities.

A natural outcome of such museum myopia had a significant impact on collecting. An enormous segment of the art-producing universe was missing. Finally the problem is being rectified. Museums are taking corrective action to acquire art that encompasses a more comprehensive, and thus honest, representation of imagery being made by individuals and groups previously shunned, whether consciously or accidentally. To say the least the results are exciting and promising as excellent art is being sought, exhibited, studied, and acquired. The future of the new collecting has also shown that quality is not sacrificed. Marvelous and excellent work is being accepted into museums and will be meaningful going forward. This chapter explains how creative even smaller museums can be in expanding an acquisition scope to get superb new art that in the past would have been missed and lost.

Introduction

As noted throughout this book, there are commonalities in the process of acquiring art among American museums as well as many individual approaches. This is especially true during periods of economic challenges such as the Great Recession that began in 2008 and the recent loss of revenue streams resulting from the COVID-19 pandemic in 2020. Even if institutions have dedicated endowments for acquiring art, these funds are at the whims of market forces. Additionally, many museums often have greater difficulties raising money for contemporary art acquisitions in times of economic downturns than in prosperous periods. Shrinking acquisition funds and the expansion of the contemporary art market often exclude many museums, especially small, mid-sized, and regional ones, from adding current works of art to their collections. As a result, many museums have

DOI: 10.4324/9781003216384-4

begun to evaluate their collections and acquisition policies and to implement creative and entrepreneurial strategies.

In addition to the contractions in the economy that often affect museum acquisition budgets are the growing costs associated with purchasing contemporary art. Art economist Olav Velthuis explains:

> Here is the math: Since the mid- [19]80s, the most expensive contemporary works of art . . . have on average increased eighteen times in price. In the same period, the average per capita income in the United States, the richest country in the world, tripled. The most coveted works of contemporary art, in other words, have become six times less affordable, which is to say, the wealth needed to buy these works has increased dramatically.
> (Velthuis 2008: 308)

He continues: "Contemporary art is receding toward a kind of commercial sublime, barely accessible to all but a very few" (Velthuis 2008: 308). To combat these market challenges and to continue adding art to their permanent collections that expand the art historical context and critically engage with our world in the twenty-first century, museums need to be innovative in their acquisition efforts. This chapter examines how the Birmingham Museum of Art (BMA) in Birmingham, Alabama, used creative and collaborative efforts to add two important contemporary works of art to their permanent collection: Kerry James Marshall's *School of Beauty, School of Culture*, 2012, and Fred Wilson's *Old Salem: A Family of Strangers*, Series One, 1995.

First, to purchase the Marshall work, the BMA made this acquisition an institutional priority by combining funds from many sources – including collector group dues, individual donations, and money from fundraising efforts – all matched 50/50 with general acquisition funds originally earmarked to cover other departmental needs. Second, for the Wilson work, the BMA opted to co-acquire and share the work of art with another institution. These two approaches to acquisitions – while not completely new – tell a story of how museums are adapting to a changing marketplace and the higher costs for contemporary works of art. With information gathered from conversations with the BMA's current and former directors and curator involved, these case studies highlight the necessity of small, mid-sized, and regional institutions to maintain and cultivate strong relationships and social networks to expand their limited resources, especially when it comes to collecting contemporary art.[2]

Kerry James Marshall's *School of Beauty, School of Culture*, 2012

Patrons are the lifeblood of museums; by investing their time and financial resources, they often aid museum acquisition efforts. The formation of patron and collector groups is often key in fostering a collector base that supports a museum in multiple ways. With such collectives, the institution provides education and connoisseurship programs, including arranging studio visits with artists, excursions to see important art world events such as fairs and biennials, exclusive behind-the-scenes tours at museums, and special invitations to view other private collections throughout the year. By engaging patrons – both financially and socially – a museum cultivates links with individuals who feel invested in the institution. As they continue to learn about art and begin to collect art or expand their collections, these patrons become more involved in other museum activities and become ambassadors for the museum in the community. Furthermore, as the relationship between the patron and museum grows stronger, many of the pieces collected by the individuals may, at some point, become gifts to the museum. These patrons also become valuable resources for museums in the expansion of their acquisition funds.

The BMA relies on its six different affiliate groups for acquisitions. An encyclopedic museum, its holdings include both fine and decorative arts from around the world, dating from ancient to contemporary times. With six different departments – Asian, Decorative Arts, African, Pre-Columbian and Native American Art, European Art, and Modern and Contemporary Art – acquisition funds need to stretch far. The BMA's collector groups have become valuable resources that augment existing acquisition funds consisting of several endowments.

The group for contemporary art, the Collectors Circle for Contemporary Art, began in 1991 with three passionate women who wanted to bring more contemporary art opportunities to Birmingham. The BMA recruited like-minded individuals and others who thought it would be fun to learn more about contemporary art. Members pay dues, at a rate of $500 per person, and in return are offered opportunities to travel with curators who introduce the members to dealers and artists. The group also travel to art fairs, and every year their funds are used to acquire art for the museum. Gail Andrews, former R. Hugh Daniel Director of the Birmingham Museum of Art, suggested why this aspect is so important:

> It's building the Museum's collection, but it's the fun of voting, it's seeing the material that's coming in, and they want to be able to do that over dinner every year. The people who have been in membership recruitment say that, if somebody can't travel or take some of the trips throughout the year, it's the voting that they look forward to.

The BMA's Collectors Circle is an active partner in acquiring art, although the curators and the director select the works that coincide with the museum's collection plan. Over the years, the Collectors Circle for Contemporary Art has grown into a progressive and knowledgeable group of collectors that has made several exciting and important acquisitions. However, there are still works of art that are out of the financial reach of Collectors Circle and that other acquisition funds cannot cover. To compensate for this, several years ago the BMA struck upon a new strategy: to focus on one acquisition as an institutional priority and combine funds from many sources, including collector group dues, individual donations, and money from additional fundraising efforts, matched 50/50 with general acquisition funds.

This strategy arose after each of the six curators presented a five-year collection plan to the director. Andrews explained:

> We have very little acquisition funds; we have two separate funds, and neither one is enough to do enough for all six departments at any one moment. They can't be conjoined for various reasons. [. . .] So, the six departments did curatorial plans, five-year plans [asking]: what are the priorities of the collection? What are its strengths? What are some areas of weakness where we want to build? What are some private collections that we think will be coming to us where maybe we don't spend as much time? And we continue to work with these collectors and encourage them to give things to us and bequeath things to us. Within that, everyone has these priorities, and never enough money to do all of them. So, [the question was] "what if the six departments come together and decide as a group with Gail on institutional priorities?" which is what we did. And everyone put their top two or three choices, [stating] this is what I'm looking for, and this is what I'd need and why.

The institutional priority purchase strategy was first implemented in 2010 when the former curator of modern and contemporary art brought forward artist Kerry James Marshall as his top choice, and the rest of the curators, along with Andrews, agreed.

Born in Birmingham, Alabama, in 1955, Marshall moved to Watts, Los Angeles, as a child. Both locales had a profound influence on his art. He has stated:

> You can't be born in Birmingham, Alabama in 1955 and grow up in South Central [Los Angeles] near the Black Panthers headquarters, and not feel like you've got some kind of social responsibility. You can't move to Watts in 1963 and not speak about it. That determined a lot of where my work was going to go.
>
> (Art 21 2001)

A recipient of the MacArthur Fellowship in 1997, among other awards, Marshall explores Black identity and issues of race through a variety of media. He is best known for his large-scale paintings that recontextualize Black subjects within the art historical canon and imbue them with a sense of humanity and power. In 2016 the Metropolitan Museum of Art in New York and the Museum of Contemporary Art, Los Angeles co-organized the traveling retrospective, *Kerry James Marshall: Mastry*. Numerous museums collect his work, including the Museum of Modern Art, New York; the Metropolitan Museum of Art, New York; the Walker Art Center, Minneapolis; the National Gallery of Art, Washington, D.C.; the Los Angeles County Museum of Art; and the Museum of Contemporary Art Chicago, among others (Jack Shainman Gallery 2014). The BMA first introduced Marshall's art to its audiences in 2003 by hosting a traveling solo exhibition of his work, *One True Thing: Meditations on Black Aesthetics*. While the exhibition was on view, the artist visited and led workshops. The success of the exhibition and the community response solidified the BMA's belief that it was important to add one of his large-scale paintings to its permanent collection. Furthermore, as Andrews noted, Marshall's work addresses several key issues:

> We have focused on buying work by African American artists since I've been the director.[3] Kerry James Marshall hit all those bells: collecting the arts of Alabama was very important, work by African American artists, and art that talks about the Civil Rights Movement – and while the beauty salon, *School of Beauty, School of Culture* doesn't directly address that, it does [address it] obliquely. So [because of] all of those things, it became the obvious choice.

In their collection, the BMA already had an important sculpture and several works on paper by Kerry James Marshall, but the curators felt it was important to add a major painting, as that is the medium for which he is best known. Several years before the BMA decided to make this acquisition an institutional priority, it had unsuccessfully tried purchasing a Marshall painting. Explaining the difficulties facing many museums in the attempt to acquire works by an in-demand artist, Andrews shared this insight: "We always just missed it, everything sold out, or things were already committed, already promised. As it happened, several of us were in New York for the opening of the Kerry James Marshall show. We picked a painting and we loved it and it went somewhere else." This type of scenario often occurs because few museums can make immediate commitments at an opening, whereas private collectors can. Furthermore, many galleries have waiting lists for popular artists' pieces and presell works before the openings of their gallery shows. If a gallery is unaware of a museum's interest, or if the museum is not of the perceived caliber of some of the interested private collectors, that museum might not even make it on the list.

After deciding that acquiring a major Marshall painting would be an institutional priority, the BMA's curator of modern and contemporary art began serious conversations with Jack Shainman, Marshall's dealer. Shainman offered to work with the artist and provide the BMA with the right of first refusal on Marshall's next painting. For the BMA, this was a great opportunity, but one that required a new way of finding funds. Andrews explained: "The price was a very generously negotiated price. A substantial discount for us, which was great, but it still was going to be a fundraising challenge." It became feasible only through several measures that the new strategy of institutional priority envisioned. First, this acquisition drew on a policy already in place at the BMA for major purchases wherein half of the cost comes from their general acquisition funds and fundraising covers the other half. What was new about this particular acquisition was the variety of fundraising efforts that took place. First, the curator and Andrews brought the possibility of making this acquisition before their support group, the Collectors Circle, during their annual voting acquisition event. Members of the Collectors Circle have a say in which acquisitions their dues – amounting to about

$50,000 that year – will finance. That year, the Marshall painting (presented in abstract terms, since the artist had not yet completed the work) was one of three options that also included photographs by a Birmingham-based artist and Polaroids by Andy Warhol. Andrews recalls that despite the Marshall painting being in an unfinished state, it won by a considerable margin and that people were enthusiastic about it. This was a popular event, and those members unable to attend could vote online by proxy. Information about each of the works was available before the event for people to access.

However, as there was no image to consider, promoting the possible acquisition of a Marshall painting was an inherent challenge. The option consisted of voting for the first right of refusal for a work that did not yet exist. The fact that the group chose the painting was likely due to Marshall's growing reputation and that many wanted to be part of bringing such a work to the museum. Furthermore, it demonstrated not only the faith the Collectors Circle had in the BMA's curators and directors but also their progressive thinking and ambitious attitude toward collection building. This is typical of the supporters of the BMA. The funding necessary for the Marshall acquisition extended beyond the contribution from the Collectors Circle, and Andrews and her curator found other sources that were also willing to take a leap of faith. Another affiliate group, the Sankofa Society: Friends of African American and African Art,[4] also decided to donate funds towards the acquisition. Nevertheless, raising the rest of the money needed was more difficult and required asking individuals to contribute. The museum received several $10,000 gifts and one of $25,000, but Andrews recalled that it was not easy and that

> fundraising had slowed; we got to about $100,000 and we needed more money, and we had a bequest from a wonderful woman who was a long-time supporter of the Museum. She was a painter herself, and it became so clear that she would have loved to have supported this artist [Marshall]; she loved contemporary art, she loved learning, she was great. She was in her 90s when she died, and she gave us a bequest to finish it off; that took us up over two hundred [thousand dollars].

This bequest, alongside the other financial gifts, was combined with general acquisition funds to secure the artwork. Although the BMA wished to keep the final purchase price confidential, other analogous works by Marshall during the period of the acquisition brought in high sums at auction. For example, in May 2011, *The Lost Boys*, 1993, sold at Christie's for $530,500. Three years later, on November 13, 2014, Marshall's painting *Vignette*, 2003, also sold at Christie's for $1,025,000, almost twice its estimate (Christie's). Although auction prices are often higher than purchasing from a gallery, these prices both demonstrate the demand for Marshall's work and provide a sense of the market value. The process of raising the necessary funds at the BMA took over two years – about the length of time the artist needed to complete the painting, *School of Beauty, School of Culture*, 2012.

After its completion, the work first went on display at the Vienna Secession in Austria in 2012 – adding to its provenance – and then debuted at the museum in early 2013 to great acclaim. Since that time, the painting has become a "community touchstone" according to Andrews. For example, *School of Beauty, School of Culture* inspired a pop-up wedding between a local barber and hairdresser in front of the painting at the museum. Andrews feels that the public's embracing of the work demonstrates another reason why its inclusion is important for the BMA's permanent collection. She stated, "For the community who may be walking into the Museum for the first time this painting does exactly what Kerry James Marshall intends, with how he is putting people of color in major history paintings in museums." She sees that including works like this in the collection and keeping it on view connects with many of the people of Birmingham, which is part of the museum's mission. Andrews believes that it is important to show "our engagement with the public and how we are committed to being open, we're committed to being a community hub; we're committed to education and various initiatives." Graham Boettcher, the BMA's current director, also emphasizing the importance of the work to the community, states,

> The painting has proven to be one of the most perennially popular in the Museum's entire collection. It is so beloved that when it was touring the country in two different exhibitions between 2016 and 2018, visitors noticed it was missing from the galleries and asked when it would return. Because we continue to receive so many requests to borrow this work from other museums

Figure 3.1 Kerry James Marshall. *School of Beauty, School of Culture*. Acrylic and glitter on unstretched canvas. 108 × 158 in. (274.3 × 401.3 cm). Collection of the Birmingham Museum of Art; Museum purchase with funds provided by Elizabeth (Bibby) Smith, the Collectors Circle for Contemporary Art, Jane Comer, the Sankofa Society, and general acquisition funds, ©Kerry James Marshall, Photography by Sean Pathasema

in the United States and abroad, we've had to put a short-term moratorium on lending it so that *School of Beauty, School of Culture* will remain "at home" for the people of Birmingham to enjoy.

Because of the cost of *School of Beauty, School of Culture*, it was important for the museum to find creative strategies that enabled them to acquire this painting. The approach the BMA employed of acquiring one work as an institutional priority is one it will continue to use in the future. The museum found that this method allows them to acquire works beyond their usually limited acquisition funds. In terms of contemporary works of art, however, this approach will only be useful every several years, as each of the different departments will have an equal chance to acquire works. Andrews stressed the importance of this strategy among other initiatives:

> The prices are so difficult today and that there are a couple of strategies. One, continue to court collectors because they are so important to building our collection. Try to catch artists on the way up before they go crazy – and you will have some misses along with the hits. And, yes, I do think this is a strategy [that of institutional priority] that we will continue to implement; and the strategy of taking half from the general fund and raising the rest. Because with some of the prices, some things will be unobtainable for us. Wrapping all of our acquisition funds around one purchase – it may take a couple of years – that is okay. I am much more about getting a singular great piece than getting ten things. It is not that we need more, we need the best quality, the best examples.

Boettcher reiterates this notion, stating that if the BMA did not act when it did, it would have missed the opportunity to acquire an important painting by Marshall, as his works are currently priced significantly higher. This illustrates how important it is to "catch artists on the way up," as Andrews noted, before prices for their work make them unobtainable. This is not always possible, and there are always regrets about missed opportunities: Andrews cited Carrie Mae Weems (American, 1953) and Kara Walker (American, 1969) as two artists that she wished the BMA had acted on earlier but whose works are now likely to be inaccessible. As prices continue to escalate for contemporary works of art, these regrets may increase, persist, and grow for many museums unless they implement new ways of thinking and approaching acquisitions like the BMA.

Fred Wilson's *Old Salem: A Family of Strangers, Series One*, 1995

The practice of purchasing a work of art with another institution is gaining traction among American museums with both contemporary works of art and art from other periods. However, this solution is particularly suited for contemporary art and the various forms of media that it utilizes, as it can blunt the high prices of individual artworks. One of the first examples of co-acquiring between several museums was the 2002 joint purchase of Bill Viola's (American, born 1951) video work *Five Angels for the Millennium* (2001) by three institutions: the Whitney Museum of American Art, New York; the Pompidou Center in Paris; and Tate Modern in London. Author Jason Edward Kaufman (2004) explains:

> Co-ownership of works of art is a relatively new way for museums to buy artworks for their collection. With few major works available for purchase, and prices which are often prohibitive, [this practice] is likely to increase. There are a number of good reasons for museums purchasing works of art jointly. Not only does it increase the fundraising capacity and purchasing power, and cement stronger links between institutions, but it also helps to ensure that the work of art is kept in the public domain.

Co-acquiring a work with another institution is a strategy that the BMA employs to great effect for many of the same reasons. In 2004 Andrews attended the annual Association of Art Museum Directors meeting in Ohio and visited Carl Soloway's gallery. On view was a photographic installation by New York artist Fred Wilson (American, born 1954). At a separate time during that meeting, Kaywin Feldman, then director of the Memphis Brooks Museum of Art in Memphis, Tennessee (and current director of the National Gallery of Art, Washington, D.C.), saw the exhibition. Demonstrating that even informal relationships are essential, Andrews and Feldman discussed the piece over dinner one evening and at that moment decided to propose to their respective boards that they co-purchase the work.

Andrews and Feldman both became fans of Wilson's work after his 1992 project *Mining the Museum* at the Maryland Historical Society, produced in conjunction with The Contemporary, Baltimore. Wilson, a New York–based artist, creates work that is an interesting mix of reinstallation, institutional critique, and the reimagining of other works of art. His practice often employs diving into a museum collection and recontextualizing objects to reveal the inherent racial inequity in the collecting and displaying of museum objects. Through his works of art, Wilson questions the biases of cultural collections and exposes new truths through his reshaping of historical objects.

Recognized for his inventiveness, Wilson received the John D. and Catherine T. MacArthur Foundation Achievement Award in 1999 and represented the United States at both the Cairo Biennale in 1992 and the Venice Biennale in 2003 (Graham 2007; Pace Gallery 2014). Andrews described what excites her about his work: "He was on the vanguard of taking museums' collections and pairing them with contemporary issues; historical objects with contemporary issues in a profound and moving, incredibly moving way." The piece co-purchased by the BMA and the Memphis Brooks, *Old Salem: A Family of Strangers, Series One*, 1995, is a series of 20 photographs.

Wilson created the piece by photographing nineteenth- and twentieth-century dolls from the collection of the Museum of Early Southern Decorative Arts in Winston-Salem, North Carolina, that represent marginalized members of the

Figure 3.2 Fred William, courtesy PACE gallery; Collection of the Birmingham Museum of Art; Museum purchase in honor of David Moos, former Curator of Modern and Contemporary Art at the Birmingham Museum of Art, with funds provided by Lydia Cheney and Jim Sokol, Nicola T. Drake and Russell Jackson Drake, Howard Greenberg, Mr. And Mrs. Edgar Marx Sr. and Edgar Marx Jr., John and Nancy Poynor, Amasa Smith Jr., Robin and Carolyn Wade, Julie and Jeff Ward, and members of the Collectors Circle for Contemporary Art, 2005.15s-j

community. The artist poses each figure in traditional, formal postures found in portraiture, and through the resulting images, Wilson brings honor to those historically without a voice.

Old Salem: A Family of Strangers, Series One was an important acquisition for both institutions. The piece is an excellent representation of the artist's work and appropriate for their respective collections on multiple levels. Andrews explained: "We each were strong in photography, we each cared a lot about works by African-American artists, this southern subject matter was particularly poignant and relevant to us – around Native Americans and African Americans – and so that was a very easy, straightforward purchase." Despite it being the first time either the BMA or the Memphis Brooks had purchased a work of art with another institution, both museums' boards expressed excitement about the idea of a co-purchase. Andrews recalled that "our committee on collections each thought it was a great idea. Though neither one of us had done it before. I don't remember any hesitation on the part of our committee on collections about the dual ownership."

One of the reasons this particular piece is an ideal example of a co-purchase lies in the nature of the work itself. A series comprising 20 photographs, it would be easy to divide the works should any conflicts regarding exhibitions or ownership arise in the future. If needed, the two museums could split the photographs evenly between them. However, each museum has worked well with the other to share the piece equitably, with the entire installation mounted at each venue twice since finalizing the purchase in 2004. Furthermore, because the piece is a work on paper, it cannot be continually on view for archival and longevity concerns, which negates the possibility of either museum trying to show it all the time. The BMA's former contemporary curator explained further:

> It's a multipartite, conceptual photographic work and it works out very well. We have it when we want to show it and we are in touch enough to give them heads up. Another thing about a photograph – works on paper, you do not show them for an extended period, and you rest them. So, we have to be aware of when each other is exhibiting them, and work through when we're planning to do so.

Working together to purchase the art, then continuing to work together regarding their exhibition schedules, strengthens the bond between the two museums. Even if curators and directors move on, a tie remains between the two museums, fostering new relationships among colleagues at the different institutions. As a new practice, co-purchasing has the potential to offer new ways of working and of changing entrenched structures. By combining resources and banding together, museums can challenge the hierarchies and inequalities of the art world to create something that is more sustainable. This model of merging funds not only allows institutions more leverage in the marketplace, it also promotes the sharing of more intangible resources. For example, when two museums acquire a work together, one museum plays the role of "connector," introducing the other museum to the dealer and facilitating a new relationship that will continue in the future. Additionally, when museums share a work of art, they may also join in other ventures together such as educational programming relating to their shared work of art.

Conclusion

This chapter has explored two different successful strategies at use at the BMA that combat escalating prices for contemporary art. Certainly, there will always be competition for works of art between private collectors and museums, large and small. However, as collecting for future generations is central to the mission of an institution, it must seek creative ways to continue to grow its collections. The analysis of these models – of strategically allocating funds and working with patrons through collection groups, as well as jointly purchasing with other museums – illustrates how vital it is to rely on more than one museum's resources. Instead, museums, especially small to mid-sized institutions, must look beyond their own walls, utilizing their networks to make purchases that otherwise would be out of their reach and push their acquisitions budgets much further.

Acknowledgments

This chapter would not have been possible without the cooperation of my colleagues at the Birmingham Museum of Art: Gail Andrews, former R. Hugh Daniel

Director; Graham Boettcher, current R. Hugh Daniel Director; and the former Hugh Kaul Curator for Contemporary Art, who wishes to remain anonymous. I appreciate their willingness to speak freely and share information with me on several occasions between 2011 and 2020.

Notes

1 This chapter is adapted from a doctoral dissertation by the author, submitted to the Department of Museum Studies at the University of Leicester, UK, 2015.
2 All quotes from Gail Andrews, Graham Boettcher, and curators at the Birmingham Museum of Art are taken from a series of ongoing conversations with the author that occurred in 2011, 2014, and 2019–2020.
3 Andrews was the director of the BMA from 1996 to 2017.
4 The BMA redesigned some of its support groups, and the Sankofa Society no longer exists in its previous form.

Bibliography

Abbé-Decarroux, F., Towse, R. & Khakee, A. 1992, *Cultural Economics*, Springer-Verlag, Berlin.
Altshuler, B. 2005, *Collecting the New: Museums and Contemporary Art*, Princeton University Press, Princeton, NJ.
Appadurai, A. 1986, 'Introduction: Commodities and the Politics of Value', in A. Appadurai (ed.) *The Social Life of Things: Commodities in Cultural Perspective*, Cambridge University Press, Cambridge, pp. 3–63.
Art 21 2001, 'Kerry James Marshall'. Available from: www.pbs.org/art21/artists/kerry-james-marshall [18 July 2014].
Belk, R.W. 2001, *Collecting in a Consumer Society*, Routledge, London.
Bellini, A., Alemani, C. & Davies, L. (eds.) 2008, *Collecting Contemporary Art*, JRP|Ringier, Zurich.
Benhamou-Huet, J. 2001, *The Worth of Art: Pricing the Priceless*, Assouline, New York.
Buck, L. 2004, *Market Matters: The Dynamics of the Contemporary Art Market*, Arts Council England, London.
Christie's Sales Results. Available from: www.christies.com/lotfinder.
Codignola, F. 2003, 'The Art Market, Global Economy and Information Transparency', *Symphonya, Emerging Issues in Management*, no. 1. n.p. Available from: http://webdepot.gsi.unimib.it/symphonya/RePec/pdf/symjournl52.pdf [17 May 2012].
Cuno, J.B. 2004, *Whose Muse? Art Museums and the Public Trust*, Princeton University Press, Princeton, NJ.
Frey, B.S. 2000, *Arts & Economics: Analysis & Cultural Policy*, Springer, Berlin.
Grampp, W.D. 1989, *Pricing the Priceless: Art, Artists, and Economics*, Basic Books, New York.
Graw, I. 2009, *High Price: Art Between the Market and Celebrity*, Sternberg Press, Berlin.
Heilbrun, J. & Gray, C.M. 1993, *The Economics of Art and Culture: An American Perspective*, Cambridge University Press, Cambridge.
Horowitz, N. 2011, *Art of the Deal: Contemporary Art in a Global Financial Market*, Princeton University Press, Princeton, NJ.

Hutter, M. & Throsby, C.D. 2008, *Beyond Price: Value in Culture, Economics, and the Arts*, Cambridge University Press, Cambridge.

Jack Shainman Gallery 2014, 'Kerry James Marshall'. Available from: www.jackshainman.com/artists/kerryjames-marshall/ [11 November 2014].

Johnson, K., 2007, 'The Hidden Cost of Sky-high Art Prices: Museums Are Less Likely to Acquire Major Works', *The Boston Globe*, 3 June, Boston, MA.

Kaufman, J.E. 2004, 'The Days of Single Ownership are Over', *The Art Newspaper*, vol. 147, p. 13.

Knell, S.J. 1999, *Museums and the Future of Collecting*, Ashgate, Aldershot.

McNulty, T. 2007, 'Public Museums Getting Priced Out in Quest for Art', *Pittsburgh Post-Gazette*, 16 May. Available from: www.post-gazette.com/frontpage/2007/05/16/Public-museums-getting-priced-out-in-quest-for-art/stories/200705160264 [13 July 2007].

Pace Gallery 2014, 'Fred Wilson'. Available from: www.pacegallery.com/artists/507/fred-wilson [11 November 2014].

Pearce, S.M. 1998, *Collecting in Contemporary Practice*, Sage Publications, London.

Ravasi, D. & Rindova, V. 2004, 'Creating Symbolic Value: A Cultural Perspective on Production and Exchange', *Working Paper* no. 111/04.

Rectanus, M.W. 2002, *Culture Incorporated: Museums, Artists, and Corporate Sponsorships*, University of Minnesota Press, Minneapolis, MN.

Robertson, I. 2005, *Understanding International Art Markets and Management*, Routledge, London.

Robertson, I. & Chong, D. 2008, *The Art Business*, Routledge, London.

Rosenbaum, L. 2007a, 'Art Market Fever: The Marginalization of Museums', *CultureGrrl: Blog*, 14 August. Available from: www.artsjournal.com/culturegrrl/2007/08/artmarket_fever_the_marginaliz.html [14 August 2007].

Rosenbaum, L. 2007b, 'Museums Can't Compete', *Los Angeles Times*, 4 September. Available from: www.latimes.com/opinion/la-oe-rosenbaum4sep04-story.html#page=1 [4 September 2007].

Spalding, Julian 2003, *The Eclipse of Art: Tackling the Crisis in Art Today*, Prestel, Munich.

Thompson, D.N. 2008, *The $12 Million Stuffed Shark: The Curious Economics of Contemporary Art*, Palgrave Macmillan, New York.

Thompson, D.N. 2014, *The Supermodel and the Brillo Box: Back Stories and Peculiar Economics from the World of Contemporary Art*, Palgrave Macmillan, New York.

Towse, R. & Khakee, A. 1992, *Cultural Economics*, 1st edn, Physica-Verlag, Heidelberg.

Velthuis, O. 2008, 'Accounting for Taste: The Economics of Art', *Artforum International*, vol. 46, no. 8, p. 304.

Velthuis, O. 2005, *Talking Prices: Symbolic Meanings of Prices on the Market for Contemporary Art*, Princeton University Press, Princeton, NJ.

Vickery, Jonathan 2007, 'Organising Art: Constructing Aesthetic Value', in S.J. Knell (ed.) *Museums in the Material World*, Routledge, London, pp. 214–229.

Watson, P. 1992, *From Manet to Manhattan: The Rise of the Modern Art Market*, 1st edn, Random House, New York.

Weibel, P., Buddensieg, A., Araeen, R., Volk, E. & Carey-Libbrecht, L. 2007, *Contemporary Art and the Museum: A Global Perspective*, Hatje Cantz, Ostfildern.

Weil, S.E. 1983, *Beauty and the Beasts: On Museums, Art, the Law, and the Market*, Smithsonian Institution Press, Washington, DC.

Weil, S.E. 1995, *A Cabinet of Curiosities: Inquiries into Museums and Their Prospects*, Smithsonian Institution Press, Washington, DC.
Weil, S.E. 2002, *Making Museums Matter*, Smithsonian Institution Press, Washington, DC.
Weiwei, A., Cappellazzo, A., Crow, T., De Salvo, D., Graw, I., Joannou, D. & Pincus-Witten, R. 2008, 'Art and its Markets: A Round-table Discussion – Moderated by James Meyer and Tim Griffin', *Artforum International*, vol. 46, no. 8, pp. 292–303.
Werner, P. 2005, *Museum, Inc.: Inside the Global Art World*, Prickly Paradigm Press, Chicago, IL.
White, A. 2010, *Contemporary Collecting*, M.A. & M.B.A. edn, Southern Methodist University, Meadows School of Art, Dallas, TX.
Wolff, J. 1981, *The Social Production of Art*, St. Martin's Press, New York.
Wu, C. 2002, *Privatising Culture: Corporate Art Intervention since the 1980s*, Verso, New York.

4 Collecting Period Rooms
Frank Lloyd Wright's Francis W. Little House

Morrison H. Heckscher

"Collecting Period Rooms: Frank Lloyd Wright's Francis W. Little House" by Morrison H. Heckscher, excerpted from *The Chase, The Capture: Collecting at Metropolitan Museum of Art* by Thomas Hoving. Originally published by The Metropolitan Museum of Art, New York. Copyright © 1975. Reprinted by permission. *The Chase, The Capture: Collecting at the Metropolitan*, The Metropolitan Museum of Art, 1975, pp. 207–217.

In 1972 the Museum purchased a large living room designed by Frank Lloyd Wright for a house built in Wayzata, Minnesota, between 1912 and 1915. It is the most important of the several American rooms, staircases, and other parts of buildings acquired in recent years for installation in the new American Bicentennial Wing. The use by museums of period rooms – whole rooms taken from historic buildings and reinstalled with appropriate, contemporary furnishing – has always provoked debate among museum curators, architectural historians, and preservationists. The causes of concern are not far to seek.

Period rooms require a permanent and inflexible commitment of space within a museum, they are costly to install, and they do not provide as good visibility for the objects shown in them as do regular museum galleries. On the other hand, the period room does what nothing else in a museum can do: it provides a visually and spatially appropriate setting for the chosen works of art. Objects that may seem nearly meaningless by themselves can be understood in their original context. Furthermore, the period room can be the means of preserving at least a portion of an important building that is being demolished.

Our decision to acquire the Wright room, however, was not based upon those criteria so much as upon the special character of the existing collections of the American Wing. To explain the nature of these collections a little history is in order.

For the first forty years of its existence, from 1870 to 1910, the Metropolitan was deeply involved with modern American art. Decorative arts, including glass by Tiffany and furniture by the best New York firms, was displayed in line with the Museum's stated intention to improve the quality of our domestic manufactures.

DOI: 10.4324/9781003216384-5

All this changed with the city-wide Hudson-Fulton Celebration of 1909. The contemporary arts fell from favor, and the colonial period came to the fore. At the instigation of Henry Watson Kent, the Museum's Assistant Secretary, and Robert Deforest, Vice-President of the Board of Trustees, the Museum mounted a major loan show of colonial portraits, antique furniture, and silver. It was an instant success. Even though the Director, Edward Robinson, did not think these American things were worthy of the museum (a sentiment still occasionally voiced, by the way), key members of the Board thought otherwise. Only the crowding of the objects onto platforms in our large galleries bothered them. Accordingly, it was decided that the domestic arts required suitable domestic settings for their proper permanent display. The answer was to use period rooms taken, either in whole or in part, from seventeenth- and eighteenth-century American houses. Thus, the idea of our American period rooms was born, and our approach to American decorative arts was fundamentally altered.

The search for rooms, as well as for the collections that they were to house, began in 1910. The quest intensified after DeForest became President of the Board in 1913 and encouraged it. By the early 1920s portions of more than twenty rooms, some of great architectural importance, had been collected. In 1922 Mr. and Mrs. DeForest themselves gave funds to build a new wing that had been designed to house the collection. In 1924 the American Wing was opened, and, ever since, it has been one of the most popular parts of the museum.

Opening off the central gallery on each of three floors were eighteen old rooms, suitably furnished, dating from the seventeenth to the early nineteenth century. The idea behind these rooms changed during the decade of collecting woodwork and its final installation in the American Wing. Elements that had originally been acquired as sympathetic backgrounds were now considered works of art themselves.

During the next forty years more rooms were acquired, but they served to improve and refine the existing collection rather than to enlarge the scope. The only architecture and decorative arts thought to be collectible were those made prior to about 1815, before the advent of industrial mechanization. The problem was not just a matter of taste. With all those eighteenth-century rooms, it was impossible to make space in the existing wing for objects, much less rooms, of the later nineteenth century. With no reasonable expectation of ever being able to house works from the nineteenth century, the Museum simply did not collect them.

In the mid-1960s the picture changed. James Biddle, Curator of the Wing, began a drive to enlarge its space. By 1967 the conception of a vastly bigger American Wing was on paper at least as Museum policy. The old wing was to stay as the core of the new building. After fifty years, beloved by a wide public, it has become, itself, a historical monument.

The existence of the rooms representing American architecture up to 1815 left the staff little choice except to continue the collection through the nineteenth and into the twentieth century. Otherwise it would appear that we regarded the architecture of the Victorian period as unworthy of representation.

With real prospects for a new building, the department began to collect the arts of the nineteenth century with conviction. The Museum's centennial exhibition, *19th-Century America*, also gave us the chance to preview some of our new rooms. Berry B. Tracy, the Wing's new curator, using woodwork acquired for permanent installation in the future Wing, created five temporary period rooms representing significant architectural styles up to 1870.

But this exhibition, splendid full dress rehearsal though it was, demonstrated some weaknesses in the American Wing's collections. The first American architects to have international significance, H.H. Richardson, Louis Sullivan, and Frank Lloyd Wright, were not represented. We were too late for Richardson; with one exception his greatest domestic interiors had been destroyed. Sullivan, a designer of commercial buildings, had never been considered. Wright's prairie houses still dotted the midwestern landscape, but they were not considered museum pieces. This was the situation when I joined the staff in 1968 as an assistant curator.

Against this background, you can imagine my interest when, in 1971, I learned that Northome, the largest summer house designed by Wright in Minnesota for Francis W. Little, was probably going to be demolished. Located far from most of Wright's other work, Northome was relatively unknown, even to architectural historians. I knew it only from photographs, which now interested me anew. My eyes were drawn to the great living room in its own almost free-standing pavilion. It was big. Henry-Russell Hitchcock called it "the most spacious domestic interior Wright had ever designed." And it was beautiful. Light poured in from long banks of pattered glass windows, and the flat-coved ceiling appeared to float above the room. But there was something more. Unlike many of Wright's domestic living rooms, this one was entirely self-contained; it did not blend spatially into adjoining rooms. It could be treated on its own. In brief, it was both spectacular and eminently suitable for installation in a museum. I tried to put that thought out of my mind. How could anyone even think of tearing down such a house?

My informant about the house and the present owners' plans for it was Edgar Tafel, a New York architect who had first been referred to me by Arthur Rosenblatt, the Museum's Vice-Director for Architecture and Planning. Tafel had been one of Wright's students at Taliesin and remained an ardent admirer of his work. He had recently restored a Wright house in Buffalo and was concerned with what might happen to Northome. Friends of his in Minnesota, including Don Loveness, another Wright buff, were keeping him apprised on developments.

I alternated between greedy admiration for that living room and absolute horror at the thought that Wright's house was going to disappear. As a curator, I saw something splendid for the Metropolitan Museum; as an architectural historian concerned with preservation, I saw defeat in demolition. It was the classic dilemma. The safest course would have been to write a couple of letters of indignant protest about the situation and wash my hands of another American tragedy. But that I didn't do. The collecting instinct won out.

The situation was this: Northome was owned by Mr. and Mrs. Raymond V. Stevenson, the daughter and son-in-law of the man for whom Wright had built it. After living in it year-round for more than twenty years, the Stevensons now found the house much too big for themselves or for any of their children. Efforts to sell it to a sympathetic private buyer had not succeeded, and local ordinances would not permit its use for anything other than a single-family dwelling. Proposals to turn it into a restaurant or a museum had been rejected as unsuited to the suburban neighborhood. The local authorities had permitted the Stevensons to begin building a new smaller house just below the big one, with the understanding that, in accord with local zoning regulation, those parts of Wright's house closest to the new building would be taken down. The closest parts were the great living room and its entrance vestibule. Obviously, if the Museum was to save anything, it would have to act fast.

In November 1971, Barry Tracy, Edgar Tafel, and I flew out to Wayzata to see what could be done. The Stevensons were most hospitable. They were also, I think, eager to meet us. Don Loveness had already discussed with them the Metropolitan's possible interest in the room. Our proposal obviously had some appeal. First, the Museum would be paying for the privilege of taking away those parts of the house that would have to be removed anyway. Second, the negative aspects of the destruction would be lessened if significant parts of the house could be saved.

The Stevensons ushered us into the room. I won't readily forget that first overwhelming impression. It was much more wonderful than photographs could portray. A sublime space, exquisitely detailed and with natural materials and soft earth colors. The room had hardly been touched since its completion in 1915. The wood trim still had its original wax finish, the plaster its original earth-tone washes; even the original furniture was still in place. And all was flooded with autumnal light. Berry and I agreed that if the house must come down, we must have the room and all its furnishing. We would install it in the new Wing with a view, through the banks of patterned glass, into Central Park.

From experience I knew that our Director's enthusiastic support would be essential for any such major acquisition. The permanent commitment of space in the new building, as well as the costs of disassembly, transportation, and installation were matters that would not be treated lightly. We were fortunate, however, that, through the munificent bequest of Emily Crane Chadbourne in 1965, funds were available for projects relating to the new American Wing building. As it turned out, Tom Hoving himself had seen Northome years before. It took only a few of Edgar Tafel's seductive color slides to refresh his memory of the room. I spoke of the Museum's long-term involvement with the American period rooms and their increasing importance in the proposed new building and noted that we had nothing to represent the major architects of the end of the nineteenth century. The Northome living room, I concluded, would give our collection of American rooms something of international stature. And with it we could obtain the original furniture and even some of the architectural drawings and correspondence dealing with the design and construction of the house. Hoving agreed that we should buy the room.

Now, a question arose. If the Museum bought the great room, what would happen to the rest of the house? It contained a library and three bedrooms, each eminently adaptable for museum use, as well as some 200 casement units of ornamental "leaded" glass. The glass had good market and would probably be saved, come what might. The rooms were something else; they would most likely be destroyed. In the end it was decided that the Museum should offer to buy the whole house and salvage all the glass and finish trim. The extra rooms and glass would be offered to other museums, and the proceeds would help cover the costs of salvage. Though temporarily burdensome, this course of action would best assure the proper disposition of all the elements. It might also reduce some of the criticism the Museum would inevitably get for being associated with the demolition of a Wright house.

The Stevensons, going ahead with building of their new house, wanted a quick decision. In December, Tom Hoving, Arthur Rosenblatt, and I flew to Minneapolis. We arrived at Northome, met the Stevensons, and went to the room. I didn't have to say a word.

Later we met with the Stevensons and their lawyer. In an hour all was settled. The Museum would purchase the entire house but not the land on which it stood. The house would be dismantled in the spring or summer, as soon as the Stevensons had moved into their new one. It was decided that the transaction should not be immediately publicized. While the Stevensons had always tried to make the house available to visitors with a genuine interest in Wright's work, the quantity of rubberneckers was growing all the time. The house was becoming unlivable.

I flew back to New York with a paper shopping bag stuffed with drawing and correspondence related to the building of the house. Some of these documents I had seen before; others Mrs. Stevenson had found recently, after learning of my interest in every scrap of documentation. These papers were rich with suggestions of the tension between the strong-willed client and the strong-willed architect who together had created Northome. Such records would be priceless in our efforts to make the room come alive in the Museum.

In New York the Trustee Acquisition Committee was chitted for approval of the transaction, and it was granted. With the chase completed, excitement ebbed, and we realized that the work had just begun.

The first priority was that the house be properly recorded before its demolition. In January 1972 I accompanied an appraiser to Wayzata. He listed and described all the important interior architectural elements and all of the original furnishings, as well as some additional Wright-related books and drawings I had found. The temperature outside, as we did our recording, was –15, and in the great room it must have been near zero. Ball-point pens froze. At the end of two days, job done, I left Wayzata with a cold that wanted to qualify as pneumonia.

The next task was to make measured drawings and a full set of record photographs of the house. We waited for warmer weather. In March, Kevin Roche and John Dinkeloo Associates, the Museum's architects and the firm that would ultimately incorporate parts of the house into the American Bicentennial Wing, sent a three-man team to do that job.

On my several visits to Wayzata I had gotten to know the Stevensons quite well. They had grown very interested in our plans for installing the room in New

York. Now they wanted to have a last great party in the house and to invite, rather as guests of honor, Tom Hoving and other members of the Museum's staff. On Friday the 12th of May, Northome was at its most beautiful. Two hundred people moved effortlessly in and around what was now our great room. It worked wonderfully well with a large crowd. Except for our Museum contingent, the Stevensons' guests were family, friends, and neighbors. At least three of them, during the evening, expressed their pleasure to me about the transaction that had solved the Stevensons' problem and then asked *sotto voce*, "But what is it about this old house that is of interest to your Museum?" Looking at the room around me, I realized that we still had a lot of eyes to open.

The final bittersweet day came in June. On the day that demolition began Ada Louise Huxtable, in the *New York Times*, reviewed our purchase as "one of the most important acquisitions in the field of American art by any museum."

5 A New Museum Builds a Collection

How One Gift Leads to Others: James A. Michener Museum of Art's Acquisition Success

Bruce Katsiff

Collections define museums. Think of a museum, and one or more of its acquisitions can pop into your mind's eye. For the Louvre it might be Leonardo da Vinci's *Mona Lisa* painting. The Smithsonian Institution in Washington, D.C. has the Wright brothers "Flier," the first successful airplane. Chicago's Field Museum of Natural History boldly exhibits "Sue," which is arguably the world's most famous *Tyrannosaurus rex* skeleton.

But how does a museum become known for a particular collection or collection focus? This chapter provides an excellent explanation of how that happened for one museum when it was created. The James A. Michener Art Museum is in Doylestown, Pennsylvania, not too far north of Philadelphia. A key assignment for founding director Bruce Katsiff was to establish a signature collection appropriate for the museum that was feasible to acquire. The museum is located in a community known today as the home of the Pennsylvania Impressionists. This loosely knit group of men and women painters was attracted to the area in the early twentieth century because of its beauty along the Delaware River, the unique visual quality of its well-established family farms nestled in the rolling cultivated hills, and its affordability and ease of access from both New York City and Philadelphia, America's preeminent art centers at the time. Bruce explains the fascinating story of how he and an incredible team of enablers were able to establish the Michener Museum as the singular institution devoted in large part to preserving that unique national heritage.

In 1989, after a 25-year career as a fine arts photographer and professor of photography, I accepted the position of director of a very young arts organization, the James A. Michener Art Center in Bucks County, Pennsylvania, a suburb of Philadelphia. With a population of just under 650,000, the county has a long and deep artistic tradition, and the center was bolstered by the remaining portion of the 23-foot-high wall that originally surrounded the prison. The site was also across the street from the Mercer Museum with its impressive, nationally important collection of material culture, installed in one of the first buildings built as a museum in America and next door to a new county regional library visited by thousands

DOI: 10.4324/9781003216384-6

annually. Just a short walk from Doylestown's historic and attractive downtown, the complex was to become the cultural center of Bucks County.

There was another important asset: James A. Michener, the institution's namesake. Michener, a foundling and native son, grew up in Doylestown and became a well-known and respected writer in the second half of the twentieth century. After winning the Pulitzer Prize for *Tales of the South Pacific* in 1948, Michener went on to write over 40 books, many of which were turned into popular Hollywood films. Michener was a dedicated human rights activist, who through his writings, taught America about racial and ethnic diversity at a time when much of our country was not interested in the subject. The musical *South Pacific*, which was based on Michener's book, was banned in South Africa in 1964 because it explored the issue of interracial marriage.

There were, however, two essential elements missing in this picture needed to create a successful museum. First, an appropriate facility needed to be built that would meet accepted national standards for museum buildings, including climate controls, attractive galleries, storage facilities, and public spaces. Second, although the institution had a modest collection composed of fewer than 250 objects, a meaningful collection that had a significant relationship to the community had to be acquired. Constructing the building was the easy part; with a successful capital campaign and a talented architect, a new facility was created to house the James A. Michener Art Museum, its name changed from Center to Museum to reflect its evolving mission.

Figure 5.1 Michener Art Museum, Photo by James Quinlan. Image courtesy of the James A. Michener Art Museum

But a museum without a meaningful collection is a hollow shell. The story of how the collection was started and built is more complex, more interesting, and was much more challenging.

Jim Michener was not only a famous and enormously successful author; he was also a skillful and disciplined collector whose creative approach both to collecting and to philanthropy made the museum's first major acquisitions leap possible. In the 1950s he began to build two separate personal collections. The first effort was an outgrowth of his interest in Japanese culture. He started to collect Ukiyo-e prints, Japanese wood block prints with a long history dating back to the seventeenth century. Over the course of several years and with the help of a knowledgeable curator, Jim assembled a collection of over 5,000 prints and wrote a book about the history of this artistic tradition called *The Floating World*. Jim also started buying American paintings by living contemporary artists. Over a ten-year period, he amassed a second collection of almost 300 twentieth-century American paintings. Again, proceeding with a disciplined approach, spending $75,000 per year and not spending over $5,000 for any individual painting, he would purchase the works directly from the artists whenever possible. Either collection would have been a galactic start for the young Michener Museum, but both collections had already been given to two other museums. The Japanese prints were given to the Honolulu Academy of Art, and the paintings were given to the Blanton Museum of Art at the University of Texas at Austin.

Unlike many other collectors, driven by his personal approach to collecting, Jim had given away both of his collections to public institutions soon after completing them. He saw his major objectives as learning through the collecting experience and sharing the works with the general public. He undertook a careful search before deciding on the Blanton as the recipient of his collection of American paintings. He chose the Blanton because he realized that his collection, while significant, would be lost in the vast collections of a major East Coast museum like the Museum of Modern Art. In Texas, it was the finest example of twentieth-century American paintings west of New York City and east of Los Angeles. The collection was important to the Blanton and to the people living in Texas. Years later, I was to use Jim's thinking as the best argument to acquire a major collection for the Michener Art Museum.

Jim wanted to help the new museum that bore his name build a collection, but he did not believe in spending huge sums to purchase the works of dead artists to the benefit of dealers and speculators. Jim also understood a museum's desperate need for general operating income. He instead had a novel idea that addressed both of his concerns. In 1992 Jim visited the museum while its first expansion effort was under construction. Late one evening during that visit, Jim sat down with a small group of museum supporters around a table at a local restaurant after dinner. At that table he proposed a challenge grant, but not the usual type, which offered cash to be matched by cash. Instead, Jim offered to contribute $500,000 to the museum's operating endowment if the museum could secure gifts of works of art to match his challenge grant.

It was a unique and interesting idea, but the details were important and challenging. Over the course of the next several weeks, working together with staff and board members, I negotiated the fine points of the deal. The first issue was to establish a specific list of the artists whose works would qualify for this challenge. The museum was located in an area that was rich with world-class museums. In order to make a distinctive mark and to have a realistic and achievable goal, the museum had decided to focus its collecting interests on artists from the region. One important group was the Pennsylvania Impressionists, who were active in Bucks County in the first half of the twentieth century. But many other artists with different styles were also tied to the community. Twenty-two well-known deceased artists from the region were specifically identified as those whose works would qualify for the match.

The original idea about how to verify that the challenge was met was to determine the value of the donated objects, with the requirement that the total value of the donated artworks equal $500,000. It became clear that this approach had many serious flaws. The museum would need to have all the donated works appraised to determine their value, which would not only be costly but also had the chance of potential disagreements between the donor and the museum about the value of the works. It might also run afoul of the IRS regulations prohibiting museums from providing appraised values to donors. To avoid these problems, it was decided that 40 museum-quality works would meet the challenge. The next issue was determining if the offered object was of museum quality and confirming to Jim that the 40 gifts had been secured. The use of the museum's collections committee solved this problem. The committee would need to accept the gift offers, and the respected collection's committee chair, Judge Edward G. Biester, would be responsible for certifying to Jim that qualified artworks that met the challenge terms had been gifted and accepted. The final wrinkle was the question regarding drawings, prints, and other works on paper. Since it would not be honorable to allow a single print to count as one of the 40 required objects, it was decided that the judge could put together several smaller works on paper into groups and then count each group as one of the 40 required objects.

With all the details settled, the museum began its effort to acquire the needed gifts in earnest. A press release was issued, which was quickly picked up by Associated Press, and the campaign was launched, with stories about this creative and unusual challenge grant appearing across the country. A story about the Michener Endowment Challenge by art critic Edward Sozanski appeared in the September, 10, 1992 edition of the *Philadelphia Inquirer*. Michener was quoted in the story and urged prospective donors "to probe into forgotten corners to ferret out the works we need so badly. If any citizen has a work that ought to be in our pantheon of area artists, he or she should get in touch with the museum." He further stated that "nothing would make me happier than to be required to turn over the entire half million."

An early donor to the challenge exemplifies the relationship between the Bucks County community and its artist residents. Dr. D. Kenneth Leiby arrived in the local river town of New Hope in 1936, set up his medical practice, and began the life of a small-town doctor. Dr. Leiby said he delivered 2,500 babies in the river valley, and he would often barter medical services for artwork from his artist patients. Leiby was a fan of Michener and was interested in a possible gift. After several discussions the doctor agreed to donate 14 works of art, including several paintings by major figures in the Pennsylvania Impressionist movement. A story about his acquisition of a work by Henry Snell was particularly touching.

Dr. Leiby was sitting at the Snell home with Snell's wife the night the artist died in his home bedroom. When Leiby and Mrs. Snell moved into the living room, she went up to a panting hanging on the wall, lifted it off the wall, and said, "Doctor this is for Thee. Henry wanted you to have it." The painting, titled *The Barber's Shop* showed the major intersection in New Hope with the building that housed the second-floor apartment of Dr. Leiby as the central part of the composition.

In total 189 works of art, including, 44 paintings, 132 works on paper, 8 sculptures, and 5 decorative arts objects, valued at more than double the dollar value of Jim's endowment gift, were donated as part of the challenge grant. We had met and exceeded the challenge. We arranged for Michener to write personal thank-you letters to every donor, and we handed out many autographed copies of his books as thank-you presents. In February 1994, just 18 months after that late-night meeting when Jim first proposed his idea, we had completed the challenge grant and added 189 works to our collection and $500,000 to our collections care endowment. This extraordinarily successful acquisitions program became the major starting point of our collections building effort. It was an important start, but only the beginning.

Figure 5.2 Henry B. Snell (1859–1955), *The Barber's Shop* n.d. Oil on canvas, 25 × 30 inches, James A. Michener Art Museum. Michener Art Endowment Challenge Gift of D. Kenneth Leiby

One of the most significant and totally unexpected benefits of the endowment challenge happened in part because of a newspaper article about the program which appeared on June 14, 1992, in a local newspaper in Mount Alto, Pennsylvania, site of one of the Pennsylvania State University's campuses. The campus librarian and resident institutional historian, Marjorie Bluebaugh, read the story about the challenge grant and noticed that one of the artists mentioned in the article was Daniel Garber, a widely recognized Pennsylvania artist. Garber, born in 1880, started his art education in 1897 at the Art Academy of Cincinnati and then attended the Pennsylvania Academy of the Fine Arts from 1899 to 1905. He was quickly recognized as a talented student and, after graduating, traveled abroad on a Cresson Fellowship, awarded by the academy for foreign travel or study. After his return he was invited to join the faculty of the academy in 1909. In 1925 he was awarded a major commission to create a large mural painting celebrating the natural resources of Pennsylvania, which was to be installed in the Pennsylvania Building at the 1926 Sesquicentennial Celebration in Philadelphia. After the close of the sesquicentennial, the mural, which was owned by the Commonwealth, was given to the State Forestry School located in Mt. Alto.

Garber supervised the installation of the mural in the newly constructed auditorium. The mural measured 22 feet wide and 11 feet high, but the rear of the auditorium where the mural was to be installed was only 20 feet across. The mural was eventually forgotten. But luckily, Marjorie Bluebaugh, the librarian, was well aware of the mural's history. On June 15, the day after reading about the challenge grant, Margery called the museum, spoke to the switchboard operator, and left a message that said, "Penn State has a large painting done by Daniel Garber in 1926, maybe the museum might purchase it or we might donate it." Those are the kind of calls a museum director returns! After speaking with Marjorie the next day, I began to research the painting, learned something of its history, and realized quickly that this was the long-forgotten Garber Mural. On June 18, 1992, I wrote to Marjorie, informed her of our interest, and arranged to visit the campus and see the work on August 13.

Mt. Alto is about a 2.5-hour drive from the museum in Doylestown, and I arranged for two of our trustees to join me for the trip. My board chair, Carolyn Smith, a grand woman and major patron who owned the local newspapers, joined with Dana Applestein, who was Daniel Garber's granddaughter. When we arrived at the campus, we first visited Marjorie and were escorted by her into the auditorium, a modest space with around 400 wooden seats and a small stage with a typical curtain across the front. The curtain was pulled back, and we saw at the back of the stage a dark and virtually indistinguishable painting that we could hardly see. At first my heart sank, and I began to believe that our trip had been pointless. In an act of desperation, I noticed there were some large klieg lights in the back of the auditorium. I unraveled one of the cords, plugged the light into a nearby outlet, and turned the light on. I then tilted the light upward on the painting off in the distance at the back of the stage. In an instant, it was obvious that the painting still had much of its original life; it still had its color, and it had its presence.

There was no doubt this was the lost Garber Mural – we had found it with all of the magnificent life that it possessed when Garber painted it in 1926.

The years living in the back of the stage had been hard on the mural. Maintenance workers would burn holes in the canvas and drop their cigarette butts behind it. There were 19 rips in the canvas. And the ends of the mural were not to be seen. Since the painting was 22 feet across but the stage was only 19 feet wide, the ends had obviously needed to be adjusted to make it fit. At some point the university had installed a Plexiglas covering in front of the canvas to protect the painting. It would take major conservation to clean the canvas, to repair the 19 holes, and to install the work at the museum. Despite the difficulties, the mural had suffered little, if no, light damage since it was at the back of the stage and had spent most of its lifetime in darkness. I knew that the painting was important and still had the kernels of its earlier life. It would be our challenge to restore the work and share the mural with the public.

On the car trip back to the museum we talked with great excitement about the mural, realizing that there were many obstacles yet to be overcome if we were to acquire the work. By the time I dropped Carolyn and Dana off at their homes, I had made a personal commitment. This was an important picture. This was an important piece of Pennsylvania's history. This could be the visual icon of the Michener Museum's collection. And it was my job to get that picture and bring it to our museum.

One piece of good luck was the fact that the mural was given to the State Forestry School before it became a part of the Penn State system. That turned out to be a critical factor, since any property that belonged to the school before the merger with Penn State University belonged to the Mt. Alto campus and not to the main university. This meant that the campus president, Dr. Corinne Caldwell, was in a position to negotiate with me for the possible sale and transfer of the picture to the James A. Michener Art Museum. So many people played critical roles in bringing this picture back to Bucks County, and certainly Corinne Caldwell was one of the most important players, for she was a college president willing to make a decision and willing to think about the greater good of her community. We began a series of lengthy discussions which attempted to determine the fair market value of the picture and clarify the terms and conditions under which the work might be transferred to the Michener Art Museum for restoration and presentation to the public. Fortunately, Penn State's new art museum on the main campus was not interested in the mural. If they had seen its worth, the picture would never have come to the Michener Art Museum.

One of the first steps was to determine fair market value, and we called upon several appraisers and gallery owners to help. Concurrent with that effort, I needed to begin to get some sense of how much the conservation costs would be. And finally, the question remained what terms and conditions would be acceptable to Dr. Caldwell and also work for us at the Michener? As I began negotiating with Dr. Caldwell, I had no idea where the money would come from. In 1992 the Michener was a young institution with limited resources. We had just completed our first capital campaign, opened the new facility, and were struggling to pay the bills and maintain a balanced budget. Two years later, on August 8, 1994, Corinne and I signed an agreement for the transfer of the work from the Penn State Mt. Alto campus to the Michener Art Museum. Under the terms of the agreement, we made a contribution to the Mt. Alto campus to establish a scholarship for needy students in Garber's name, and they in turn transferred ownership of the picture to the Michener Art Museum.

Although museums do not like to talk about the cost of pictures, because it is part of such a good story, I will divulge that our contribution was $55,000 to endow the scholarship fund. So, where did the money come from? At this point another contributor stepped up to the plate to help the institution. Craig Lewis was a state senator whose wife, Diane Semingson, was a member of the museum's board. Years earlier during a social function, I walked through the museum with Senator Lewis, and during that walk he told me that he would like to do something significant for the museum, perhaps helping to buy an important work of art. Craig was now about to leave his position in the state senate, and I remembered our earlier conversation. I arranged to meet with him to talk about this work and its place as a part of the commonwealth's history. Impressed with the opportunity, Craig secured a legislative initiative grant in the amount of $145,000 to cover the scholarship and most of the cost of restoration and installation. It took Daniel Garber six weeks to complete this canvas. It was to take the restorers six months to bring it back to life.

The final chapter in this story involves the deinstallation of the mural from the Mt. Alto campus, the restoration of the work, and finally, its installation in the Putman/Smith Gallery at the museum. We were fortunate to hire an exceptionally skillful conservator, Barbara Buckley, to oversee the project. Barbara is the resident conservator at the Barnes Foundation, and her husband, Mark Bockroth, was the conservator at Pennsylvania Academy of the Fine Arts and now works at the Winterthur Museum. The conservation efforts were managed by our deputy director, Judy Hayman. The first step was to remove the canvas from the stage backdrop and its wooden stretchers. Once removed, the canvas would be rolled onto a specially prepared wooden drum and transported to a studio, where the conservation work would be done. It was not possible to get the canvas out of the auditorium in its stretched form since there were no exit doors large enough to allow it to pass through. You may recall that the canvas was rolled when it was transported from Garber's studio in 1926 to the Sesquicentennial building, and it must have then been rolled again to be transported to the Mt. Alto campus. There have been many grand moments in the history of this project, and good karma seems to have helped bring it to a satisfactory conclusion. One of the first questions we had was what happened to the ends of the canvas? Remember, it was 22 feet across originally, but it was installed in a 19-foot-wide space. Had the ends of the canvas been cut and removed, or had the ends been folded back, leaving the possibility of restoration? In 1926 Daniel Garber had written a letter offering his suggestions about the work's installation. Well, obviously, Mr. Garber had advised them not to cut the ends of his painting, but to fold them back. When we got the painting off the wall at Mt. Alto, we were thrilled to learn that the ends had been folded back and not cut away. Once the painting was removed from its stretcher, it was rolled onto our specially prepared wooden roller with glassine interleafing. The conservators were concerned about what might happen when the picture was wrapped around the roller, but we were greatly aided by the fact that the painting was unvarnished. That was to be of great assistance to the conservators and was to make the cleaning of the canvas much easier because varnish removal was not required.

One problem was that Barbara Buckley's conservation studio was simply not large enough to house a painting that was 22 feet across and 11 feet high. In fact, after Barbara added the additional support materials to the outside perimeter of the canvas, she was actually working on an object that was almost 26 feet across and approximately 14 feet high. We had to rent a warehouse in West Chester, Pennsylvania, near Barbara's home so that she could do her conservation work on this picture. The warehouse had to have temperature control so that the painting wouldn't freeze in the winter or overheat in the summer during the six-month conservation period. Barbara worked with a team of assistants, and it was their job to repair all of the rips and tears in the canvas, to meticulously clean every inch of the surface, and all of that cleaning had to be done with nonabrasive cleaning agents that would in no way alter the delicate color and surface of the work.

After these first parts of the restoration project were completed, we made a decision to varnish the cleaned canvas in order to protect it and to isolate the restoration work from the original painting. Then the in-painting was done to replace the losses on the surface, and a final coat of varnish was applied again over the entire painting, which by then had been restretched on a heavy-duty stretcher specially built to hold the work.

Figure 5.3 Restoration of Mural by Daniel Garber (1880–1958), *A Wooded Watershed*, 1926. Oil on canvas, 129 × 257 inches, James A. Michener Art Museum. Acquired with a Legislative Initiative Grant Awarded by Senator H. Craig Lewis. Photo courtesy of the James A. Michener Art Museum

All that remained was to move the picture back to the Michener and to install it in the Putman/Smith Gallery as a permanent part of the museum's collection. The conservators did not want to roll the canvas again because it had been difficult to stretch it and to remove the creases from the folding So, we had to find a drop frame tractor trailer that was large enough to hold the stretched mural and transport it to the museum. As for getting a work about 12 feet high and over 22 feet wide into the museum gallery, fortunately, when we built the Putman/Smith Gallery, which had 16-foot-high ceiling, we asked the architects to build an exceptionally high emergency exit which would enable us, if necessary, to bring in a large canvas. Without that doorway, which was designed to move a 10-foot object through the loading dock and onto the elevator, we would never have been able to get the mural into the building.

The final decisions involved questions about how the mural would be installed. At the Mt. Alto campus, the wooden frame was literally nailed to the canvas surface. We did not want to use that approach, so instead decided to build a false wall in front of the mural in order to create a frame in the lunette shape, or semi-circle, of the mural. When Garber painted the work, he was not about to waste any effort. He knew that the edges would be covered, and on this large canvas he only painted an inch or two beyond where the frame would cover the edge of the picture.

Finally, in 1996, we held the grand celebration, the unveiling of the Garber Mural. With a blare of trumpets, literally, and the drama of a white falling curtain, a crowd of about 175 museum patrons assembled in the Putman/Smith Gallery and watched as we revealed what has become one of the visual icons of the James A. Michener Art Museum, Garber's mural *A Wooded Watershed* had finally been returned to Bucks County, where it had been created some 70 years earlier. Just as so much of the museum's success acquiring collections was built upon on previous successes, in another unexpected and surprising way, the Garber Mural was to contribute to yet another major collection gift.

One day in 1999, when I was living in Lumberville, Pennsylvania, I began my day as I did almost every morning by stopping at the general store, picking up my mail, saying hello to my friend Gerald Gordon the owner, hearing the latest town gossip, and glancing at the morning papers. That morning, as I sat around the "muffin table" with other locals reading the *Philadelphia Inquirer*, I was drawn to the story about the sale of Suburban Cable, a regional cable television service, to Comcast Corp. for over 6 billion dollars. Suburban Cable was owned by Gerry Lenfest, who had bought the company from Walter Annenberg for 2 million dollars 25 years earlier when Gerry was an attorney working as in-house counsel for Annenberg. I knew that Lenfest was a collector who owned Pennsylvania Impressionist pictures, having learned about him from Roy Petersen, a Lambertville, New Jersey–based dealer who had sold him pictures, and from Malcolm Polis, another dealer in the genre who advised the Lenfests on their art purchases. Gerry was also at the time the chair of the board at the Philadelphia Museum of Art (PMA). That very morning, I made a commitment and told myself that I had to "get to" Gerry and seek his support for the Michener. It was yet another important path to building the Michener's collection.

In the following weeks, I talked to the museum's chief curator, Brian Peterson, and our senior development director, Carole Hurst, about how we might meet and pitch Gerry. We all did our homework and learned as much as we could about him, even hiring a donor research firm to give us a full report on his background and philanthropic history. Then we arranged a visit with him at the headquarters of Suburban Cable, where the collection hung in offices and corridors throughout the building. Gerry had decided many years earlier to buy artwork produced in the communities where he had cable customers. Bucks County was a major part of Suburban's service area, and Gerry had bought well.

As Brian and his assistant checked out the collection of 59 Pennsylvania Impressionist paintings, I sat down in Gerry's office to chat. After exchanging customary greetings, Gerry looked me in the eye and said, "I'm not going to give you any money." I was stunned by the remark and replied, "Gerry, I'm not here to ask for money." He immediately responded, "You run a nonprofit, you're supposed to ask for money!" That began a relationship that was to help put the Michener into a higher orbit by establishing a major base for our collection and offering me and the museum a treasured patron and friend. Because of his company's sale, Gerry needed to find a place for his collection. Gerry and his wife, Marguerite, lived in a modest home in Willow Grove, and the 59 paintings in the collection would not fit in their house.

Figure 5.4 Fern I. Coppedge (1898–1951), *Autumn*, n.d. Oil on canvas, 25 × 30 inches. James A. Michener Art Museum. Gift of Marguerite and Gerry Lenfest

In addition, their children had no interest in these pictures. We talked about the future of the collection and the best use of the works. Since he chaired the board at PMA, I knew that they were to be our major competitor.

Taking a page from Jim Michener's philosophy of gifting collections, my argument to Gerry was simple. I said that PMA was a distinguished institution but that the collection would mean little to them, while the gift would be transformative to the Michener. We sparked his interest, and a visit was arranged for Gerry and Marguerite to tour the museum. The Michener had recently completed its first expansion project, and the 22-foot Daniel Garber mural *A Wooded Watershed* had been acquired and installed in the Putman/Smith Gallery. The mural proved to be an important hook that helped to capture another important collector's interest. Gerry loved the mural and thought his collection would fit perfectly with the picture. We were building a reputation as a new regional museum of quality with a bright future. The Lenfest collection would be critical to our identity and credibility. If this major collection went to PMA, then what could the Michener become? I asked Gerry, knowing there were already several important Pennsylvania Impressionist canvases that lived unseen in the storage vaults at PMA, how many such paintings were hanging at PMA. He said they just didn't have enough space to put them in the galleries. I asked why, out of the thousands of paintings hanging at the museum, there wasn't room for one painting from the group. Our argument was bolstered by the lack of interest in the works by some of PMA's

Figure 5.5 Edward W. Redfield (1869–1965), *The Trout Brook*, ca. 1916. Oil on canvas, 50 × 56 inches. James A. Michener Art Museum. Gift of Marguerite and Gerry Lenfest

curators. Despite these advantages, I was up against a respected and skillful competitor, Anne D'Harnoncourt, a masterful museum director who could wrestle her competitors to the ground with velvet gloves. Gerry said he had met with Anne to discuss the gift, and she had a Garber painting hanging in her office when he arrived. He said he'd been had!

Carole Hurst was instrumental to the Michener effort. She advised me to move quickly, having sensed Gerry's desire to make a decision without hesitation. With the sale of his business, there were many details to complete, and finding a place for the collection was one that needed rapid resolution. Gerry told us that a significant endowment gift would come with the collection. He said, "People who give collections to museums should also give them money to care for the collections." We developed a proposal offering to move the entire collection to the museum as a promised gift and requested a 5-million-dollar endowment gift. When Anne got word that the paintings were likely heading to Bucks County, she made a clever counterproposal. She suggested that Gerry give 58 paintings to the Michener and only 1 picture to PMA, the best work in the collection, a large painting by Edward Redfield titled *The Trout Brook*. Gerry did not take the bait, deciding instead to keep the collection together.

The conditions of the gift were also inspired: the Michener was required to maintain a permanent exhibition of Pennsylvania Impressionist works but could as needed or as possible replace any of the Lenfest pictures with better examples of the specific artist. This was clearly a refreshing and unusual approach for

Figure 5.6 Bror Julius Nordfeldt (1878–1955), *The Pigs and the Crow*, ca. 1938. Oil on board, 27 × 33 inches. James A. Michener Art Museum. Gift of Marguerite and Gerry Lenfest

Figure 5.7 George W. Sotter (1879–1953), *Untitled* (Night Snow Scene), 1949. Oil on canvas, 26 × 32 inches. James A. Michener Art Museum. Gift of Marguerite and Gerry Lenfest

any collector making a museum gift, since so often collectors restrict the sale of works from their collection as a condition of the gift. The offer included all 59 paintings and a 3-million-dollar endowment to help care for the works. The paintings, by a who's who of Pennsylvania Impressionists, included three works by Walter Baum, three works by Fern I. Coppedge, three works by John Folinsbee, four works by Daniel Garber, two works by William Lathrop, four works by Antonio Martino, nine works by Edward W. Redfield, three works by Charles Rosen, seven works by George Sotter, three works by Robert Spencer, and many others. The endowment funded an endowed curatorial position. It was indeed a transformative gift that elevated the museum's stature, launched the museum into higher orbit, and marked the Michener as an important center for the study of Pennsylvania Impressionists, with the best collection of that school in any public institution.

The relationship with the Lenfests continued for years. Gerry would regularly offer support for museum publications, and he funded a traveling exhibition from the Michener collection. In 2006, when the Michener was raising 10 million for our third construction project, Gerry agreed to a million-dollar gift with one condition: his gift had to be matched by another million in gifts from the museum's trustees. Since the trustees had already pledged over 5 million to the campaign, Gerry's offer was a real challenge. It worked when Syd and Sharon Martin stepped

Figure 5.8 R.A.D. Miller (1905–1966), *Rooftops, New Hope*, ca. 1931. Oil on canvas. 20 × 24 in. James A. Michener Art Museum. Gift of Marguerite and Gerry Lenfest

up to the plate with a gift to match the challenge. We ultimately raised nearly 13 million in the campaign.

In 2010 Gerry opened discussion with us about another large gift. A local art dealer was talking to him about the possible purchase of a large group of pictures by another group of Pennsylvania artists known as the "New Hope Modernists." These were a group of local artists active in the first half of the twentieth century who turned away from representational landscape painting and pursued the world of abstraction and nonobjective painting. We were interested in the collection, but at the same time we were concerned about Gerry paying a fair price for these lesser-known artists. We advised him to bargain hard with the dealer in an effort to drive down the requested price for the collection. After much discussion, Gerry and the dealer agreed on a price, and the entire group of 28 paintings was added to the museum's collection as another Lenfest gift.

While the gifts to the Michener were transformative, they represented a tiny fraction of the philanthropic activity undertaken by Gerry and Marguerite. They helped museums, libraries, universities, art centers, newspapers, environmental causes, and many other organizations. Gerry's commitment to helping to build a better world was passionate and thoughtful, exemplifying the kind of creative philanthropy that helps institutions raise much more from their communities. I remember his often-repeated comment to me that "making the money was the easy part; figuring out how to give it away responsibly was a bigger challenge." Gerry was up to the challenge and succeeded in setting an example that will be admired for decades to come.

These three efforts, the Michener Endowment Challenge, the Garber Mural Acquisition, and the Lenfest gifts, formed the core of the Michener's collection. Two hundred and seventy-six works of art, all relevant to the museum's collections focus, were acquired in the first two decades of the museum's life. Those works, in turn, inspired numerous other gifts and support from public-spirited citizens who shared our dream to build a quality museum in our community. We started out on our journey to build an art museum for our community with an inspired site for the museum, the former county prison, adjacent to the regional library, and across the street from the Mercer Museum: the cultural center of our community. We built a substantial facility with climate-controlled galleries and storage facilities, public spaces, an outdoor sculpture garden, and educational classrooms. And finally, the most important but most difficult element, the collection, was assembled, completing the three pillars of any quality art museum. A site, a facility, and a collection; they can come in any order, but all three are needed for any museum. Collections building is a never-ending job of all museums, but it is always important to have a clear vision for the collection and to be certain the collection has relevance to the community the museum serves. In its first quarter-century, the Michener Art Museum achieved both objectives.

There is, of course, also a fourth pillar needed for a quality art museum: people. The three at the center of this story – Jim Michener, Corinne Caldwell, and Gerry Lenfest – stand out as people of great vision and passion who were critical to the Michener's success in building a distinguished collection. They shared a joy for art and a commitment to their community that in turn brought that community together around a museum that now protects and celebrates the extraordinary artistic legacy of Bucks County. Jim Michener was able to achieve his vision by helping the museum achieve its vision: contributing, in addition to art and money, a novel approach to philanthropy and inspiration to his fellow Bucks County residents. Corinne Caldwell brought the encyclopedic wisdom of a librarian, a love for Pennsylvania's history, and the kind of determination that gets things done. Gerry Lenfest brought a deep understanding of how philanthropy, when done in a wise and generous way, can have a positive and long-lasting impact. And, of course, the museum's staff, trustees, and many other important players brought knowledge, expertise, and talent to sustain a 20-year effort.

6 A Museum-Defining Acquisition

The Murtogh D. Guinness Collection of Mechanical Musical Instruments and Automata, Morris Museum, Morristown, NJ

Steven Miller

The Morris Museum, Morristown, New Jersey, has been a fondly enjoyed local institution since it started as a children's museum in 1913. Over the years its collections were accumulated by donation in an ad hoc manner rather than as a result of any focus or discipline. Consequently it had no reputation for any holdings of an outstanding unique nature. This was apparent when I was hired as executive director in 2001. Neither staff nor trustees were concerned about the randomness of what it owned. To the museum's credit, things were well cared for, catalogued, and presented nicely in both long-term and temporary exhibitions. The absence of any collection identity vanished with the gift of an extraordinary body of materials that tell about the start of mechanized entertainment that predicted today's ubiquitous IT entertainment universe. This chapter explains how that happened.

The most amazing and largest museum acquisition I ever made started when I answered a phone call one morning in 2002. I was then executive director of the Morris Museum in Morristown, New Jersey. A gentleman named Stephen Ryder was calling. We had met ten years before when I was director of museums at the Western Reserve Historical Society in Cleveland, Ohio. He is a collector and dealer in old music boxes and automata. The latter are hand-operated or wind-up robotic animatronic figures that mimic animal or human movements. The sorts of music boxes and automata he works with mostly date to the nineteenth and early twentieth centuries. The Historical Society had several galleries showing machines lent by a national membership organization that collected and promoted these antique forms of entertainment. When I met Steve, he was visiting to see the exhibit.

When Steve reintroduced himself by his phone call to the Morris Museum, he asked if I remembered him and our past visit. I did. It turned out he lived not far from Morristown, in Summit, New Jersey. We briefly caught up. He then explained the reason for his call. A very large and important private collection of antique music boxes and automata was being considered as a gift to a museum. It was in excellent condition, and the donation would be well-funded. The collector had died the previous year. A distinguished Manhattan law firm was handling the estate, which, for tax purposes, had been established as a foundation years prior. Steve and his younger brother Jere literally grew up with the collection.

DOI: 10.4324/9781003216384-7

Figure 6.1 Sample Exhibit Galleries for the Murtogh D. Guinness Collection of Mechanical Musical Instruments, Morris Museum, Morristown, NJ, 2008 (photo by Steven Miller)

His parents (collectors also) knew the owner. Steve's brother is one of the world's leading restorers of automata, and the two work closely together in their business. The collection was held in two townhouses on West 80th Street in New York City. I was interested.

Museums are often approached to buy or accept donations of things people think of interest to an institution. For various reasons the vast majority of such inquiries are politely declined. Usually an item or items is of no relevance to a museum's mission. Sometimes an acquisition is impractical. This would especially be the case with large things or materials in poor condition. If a sale is involved, a museum may not have the necessary funds or may not wish to find donors. Collection gift proposals occasionally have restrictions attached to them. These usually set exhibition demands, promises to never sell or otherwise dispose of the gift, and requirements for ways donors are given credit for the generosity.

During my museum career I have declined most acquisition proposals. I always see the exercise as a public relations opportunity. I explain the mission of the museum being approached, discuss current collection needs, and, if possible, always suggest alternative repositories. Some approaches are worth at least investigating beyond an initial inquiry. Given the nature of the Morris Museum's collections at the time and its programming activity, I felt Steve's approach worth discussing further.

The Morris Museum was founded in the early twentieth century as a children's museum in Morristown. In growing over the years, it had eventually moved into an unoccupied mansion a few miles from the village. Periodically the museum continued to expand that facility, even adding a 316-seat Actors' Equity theater. Though trying to be a museum for adults as well as children, it never lost the reputation as a kids' museum. The collections and exhibits reflected this schizophrenic personality. Moreover, attempts to define the place reflected an intellectual vacuum. Fortunately its fogbound mission persona seemed to have no adverse impact on its operations or audience. The community liked and respected it, especially families. The theater had a small but loyal following. There was little cross-over between the museum and theater attendees, but that bothered neither staff nor the board of trustees. The operating budget was always relatively balanced, employees were loyal, and the trustees were dutiful, if not overly generous, fiduciaries.

When I started as director of the Morris Museum, its collections presented a mystery to me. Over the years they had been gathered with little focus. The only logic I could decipher was to see them as teaching "props" for education programming. This, of course, corresponded with the children's museum origins of the institution. Museums rarely shed founding motivations. Fortunately the collections were well cared for and appropriately catalogued. It was clear the museum had never existed to preserve physical evidence of the human or natural world relevant for a targeted subject for the long term. There was no rhyme or reason to the exhibitions it presented, be they drawn from the permanent collection or temporarily borrowed. Just about anything could be shown for any reason, be it a painting, a toy, a rock, a dress, a chair, a piece of sculpture, and so on. I was pleased to see that, as with collection management responsibilities, exhibits were also well done and professional in appearance and content.

In trying to define the Morris Museum, I eventually decided it was about celebrating creativity in four disciplines: art, science, theater, and history. The concept worked well in application. We could devise an overarching emphasis on teaching when deciding how to schedule programs of all sorts, be they exhibits, activities, events, plays, and other performances. Educating in our four scholarly areas became an operating determinate. It also helped us define a collecting policy to acquire instructive examples of individual creativity. It further reflected the museum's pedagogical roots. The board of trustees never commented on this new idea of the why behind the Morris Museum's persona. In time, it began to appear in things they said at meetings, and after I retired it was heralded in all media and other public materials.

As the saying goes, "timing is everything," and that was certainly the case with Steve Ryder's call to me. The collection (and money) Steve told me about belonged to Murtogh D. Guinness (1913–2002) a scion of the Anglo-Irish Guinness brewing fortune. He was quite wealthy and had long lived an ex-patriot's life in New York City. He owned two adjoining townhouses on East 80th Street a few blocks away from the Metropolitan Museum of Art. Both houses were full of his collection. Guinness had died a year before Steve's call to me. We were unaware of any immediate family or other heirs. He did have a sister in England, the Dowager Marchioness of

Normanby. It was unknown to Steve how many friends and family might be listed in his will. Apparently there were none of consequence and little family interest in having his collection (or the townhouses). There was something of a desire to keep the collection together in a public repository if possible.

The Guinness family had long used the New York City "white shoe" law firm Kelly, Drye and Warren to handle its North American interests. It was responsible for the Murtogh D. Guinness estate settlement. Given the firm's profitable history with the Guinnesses, it was more than willing to seek a museum for Murtogh's collection and assure its care and preservation through a restricted endowment established with funds from the sale of the townhouses. But what museum would want it, and how could that be done in a timely manner? Being involved in these private discussions, Steve offered to assist the law firm. His call to me was part of that process.

Steve explained that Guinness wanted his collection to go to the Metropolitan Museum of Art upon his death. He envisioned the machines being carried from the townhouses, down the street to the museum, and up the grand front steps of the Fifth Avenue entrance as they were joyfully welcomed into its permanent collections. This was a nice sentiment. No such arrangement had been agreed to by anyone in authority for either Guinness or the museum.

Soon after Murtogh died, the director of the Metropolitan Museum of Art was invited to visit the townhouses and review the estate's bequest offer. The Met's instrument curators knew Guinness well. They had assumed his pieces would end up in their care. Upon seeing the machines, the director said the museum would not want the entire collection. The disappointed curators were instructed to select only 40 or 50 of the best items for acquisition. Murtogh's family members, and thus the estate lawyers, declined the idea. This unanticipated setback suddenly required the attorneys to scramble for other options to fulfill the desires of the deceased collector and his family.

Museums remained the most logical donation choice. The question was how to effectively solicit ideal candidates. Many private collections find museum homes, but this rarely happens in an overt public manner. Advertisements, targeted mailings, social media alerts, etc., are uncommon ways to achieve successful museum donation outcomes. Such acquisitions are handled quietly behind closed doors. Further complicating matters was the cost of maintaining the Guinness townhouses. The attorneys were in a bit of a time crunch to sell them – minus the contents!

During their careers it is not unusual for museum directors, curators, conservators, and collection managers to be asked to assess private collections for possible museum acquisition. The approaches may be for purchase, or gift, or some combination thereof. Most are hardly worth the time it takes to respond to the inquiry. In those instances initial contact is polite, if perfunctory. Museum staff expresses gratitude for a solicitor's interest. Explanations are given about the mission inappropriateness of an offer and the difficulty of facilitating such an acquisition. The less appropriate a collection is for a museum, the shorter the conversations. However, if a collection is alluring, enthusiastic discussions unfold.

After talking with Steve at length, I realized we might have an inside advantage should the Guinness machines be an acquisition target. It was decided he would ask the estate's law firm if representatives of the Morris Museum might see the collection. Steve was in the ideal position to endorse us, explain my background, and noting how we had met previously at the Western Reserve Historical Society. I authorized Steve to say that if the Guinness collection and donation terms were suitable, we would want to submit an acquisition proposal. If there were little or no interest, we would decline to pursue it.

A visit to the Guinness townhouses was arranged. It included two museum trustees, Steve, and me, as well as one of the attorneys. I selected our most difficult trustee and our most positive one. The troublemaker admired the supportive one. If the difficult man saw that his fellow trustee liked the collection, I knew progress would be far smoother should we decide to proceed with an acquisition request.

We met an estate lawyer at the townhouses at the appointed time. Once inside I was flabbergasted by what I saw. The collection was incredible. It was comprehensive and in excellent condition. Even from my limited study of the subject, it was obvious Guinness had carefully acquired the best of the best. Unlike so many weak and incomplete accumulations of things, this collection was superb in content and scope. I immediately said it had to be saved for posterity and in its entirety whether at the Morris Museum or another institution. Obviously I was rooting for us.

To my knowledge no other museum in the Americas had such an extensive and inclusive collection of machines that had once been enjoyed by all ranks of society. Historic houses often have one or two examples. Art museums have a few, acquired for the decorative craft beauty for their wood-embossed and elaborate painted cases. All the Morris Museum had was a reproducing piano, which to the untrained eye looks like a player piano device was inserted under the keys of a grand piano.

The Guinness collection represented the full range of mechanical musical entertainments once familiar to mainstream social ranks. The wealthy would have had the bejeweled lifelike miniature robotic singing birds in gold cages or in small gem-covered boxes from which they would pop up and tweet. The middle class (including my great-grandparents) would have been familiar with larger table-top music boxes displayed and played in nicely decorated nineteenth-century parlors. Daily laborers of a hundred years ago would have known the coin-operated musical devices found in every corner saloon and "free lunch" bar.

I soon learned there were museums in Europe and Japan dedicated to the sorts of devices Guinness collected. We further confirmed there was nothing anywhere in the Western Hemisphere. Receiving the entire collection would instantaneously establish the museum as a formative center for telling about the golden age of self-generated mechanical entertainment as it was seen and heard well before the electronic and digital instruments and devices so common today. The Guinness collection summarized a missing chapter in entertainment history.

We spent about two hours in the house looking, listening to, and familiarizing ourselves with the collection. It was situated all over the place, on each floor, well shown and obviously appreciated for both aesthetic and acoustic reasons. Why Guinness formed his collection remains something of a mystery, but it was clear he loved each and every item. And he was not secretive about its ownership. Virtually anyone interested in the subject could arrange a viewing and listening tour. He, in turn, sought out other collectors.

During our meeting at the Guinness townhouses, I sensed something familiar about the lawyer. I know few lawyers, so it was a puzzle. As we chatted I mentioned my museum background, which includes 16 years as a curator at the Museum of the City of New York. The lawyer said she had interned in its decorative arts office when she was in a museum studies graduate school planning a career in my field. I was there when she was, though our paths rarely crossed. Deciding a museum job was neither intellectually nor financially of interest, she changed employment plans and went into law. We therefore had an unusual bond, tenuous though it may have been.

The lawyer we met with was her firm's second in command regarding the Guinness client. Her boss, a stuffy and fussy sort, would have been a royal pain in the backside if it were not for the fact that her underling knew about museums and could explain how they operated. I was extremely fortunate throughout our negotiations. The odds of this happening are slim to none. Collection donors to museums rarely understand the inner workings of these unusual institutions.

In leaving the house I asked if I could return with two more trustees. The lawyer agreed. On that trip I took our most influential board member along with the chair of our collection committee whom the entire board deferred to regarding collection matters. The first two trustees and the second duo loved the collection. Soon after these visits we were able to have both estate lawyers come to the Morris Museum. Additional trustees met them, as well as personable staff. The museum looked good and our tour went well.

By this time there was no question in the minds of anyone at the museum now familiar with the Guinness collection that it would be an ideal acquisition. Each item reflected our new four-pronged approach to celebrating creativity in the disciplines of art, science, history, and theater. In fact, exhibitions exploring aspects of these subjects could be easily done with the machines. I even thought we could put a few in a preview exhibition identifying each with four labels: one for the science of the machine, one for the art of the machine, one for the performance of the machine, and one for the history of the machine on view. This never happened, but the information is well-contained in the permanent exhibition.

After viewing the Guinness collection and meeting with the lawyers, I asked if we could submit an acquisition proposal. The response was yes. This was in the late fall. My deadline was the end of the year. At the next meeting of the museum's trustees, I was given full authority to submit a proposal and pursue negotiations. I had no interest in making a unilateral acquisition decision and stated that clearly. The board chair was dutiful in commenting on my writing, which was then unanimously approved by the trustees before submission. In considering my acquisition proposal, I had several questions.

From our perspective, as explained to us, the terms of the Guinness gift were optimal. The successful museum "applicant" would suddenly enjoy a unique and well-funded collection renown. Institutional identity opportunities would be exciting and greatly enhanced going forward. Considering the possibilities, we assumed there would be other interested museums, but we had no idea who they might be. I had to craft our proposal to excel against unknown competitors.

We knew the Metropolitan Museum of Art was no longer a contender. We soon learned the Museum of Fine Arts, Boston wanted the collection, as did the National Music Museum in Vermilion, South Dakota. We were unaware of non-American museums possibly in the running (there were none). Apparently the Morris Museum's proximity to New York City was an advantage insofar as the Guinness family was concerned. They had no interest in seeing the collection go to South Dakota. Maybe even Boston might be a bit distant. Among other things, I would obviously highlight the value of our location in my proposal.

Another question of importance during these discussions was how quickly did the attorneys want to dispose of the collection once a donation was agreed to? Keeping it and the townhouses was costly. The lawyers had been dealt a timing blow by the Metropolitan Museum of Art's refusal to take the whole collection. Any concern on their part to move rapidly might work to our advantage if I wrote a reasonable proposal and could implement it quickly. Also, might the collection be sold if a museum home was not found? I would have absolutely no interest in purchasing any of it piecemeal. My concern was to keep the collection together for the aforementioned reasons. This could only happen at the Morris Museum if sufficient financial support accompanied the gift.

Had the acquisition been offered without the sufficient funding promised, I would have declined to pursue it. I had zero interest in organizing a campaign to get dollars to support exhibiting or caring for a collection of this magnitude and complexity. The museum had a spotty record of raising significant money for major projects. It was my sense of the current trustees that few were capable of making large financial gifts or wanted to ask for such support. This reality is explained further along in this chapter.

Internally the most important operating question I had regarding the preservation of the collection was who could care for it? A century ago there were many mechanics qualified to service and repair these machines. Those folks are long gone. Fortunately one of the best of the current restorers of automata in America is Jere Ryder. I met with him, and we agreed he could be on staff at least two days a week. His employment contract would stipulate he could not conduct any of his or his brother's private business on museum time or with museum resources. A gentleman in another New Jersey town specialized in pneumatic instrument restoration. The Guinness collection has a few. They are rather large and complicated. I met with him to ask if he might be interested in helping with the Guinness project. Happily, he had restored one of the instruments already and got along well with Guinness. Moreover, he was in good health and not too old. He agreed to help us on a contract basis, and is seen at work in my photo illustrated herein. I soon had my hands-on preservation questions about the collection well in hand.

To convince the law firm of the suitability of the Morris Museum to care for the Guinness collection in a meaningful way, it was necessary to present a cogent argument supporting the institution's professionalism not only for collections but for general operations. Concerns included our financial stability. While we had no idea what the sale of the townhouses would realize, we could establish a reasonable estimate. With those funds and others accompanying the gift, $14 million would probably be the

Figure 6.2 Alan Lightcap Restoring for Exhibition the Largest Pneumatic Musical Instrument in the Murtogh D. Guinness Collection of the Morris Museum. It Features Several Instruments. (Photo by Steven Miller.)

overall estimate for funding needed to underwrite the donation. The museum therefore set an initial budget around this number. Four million dollars would be allocated for packing and moving the collection from the townhouses to a climate-controlled secure fine art storage and work facility in Newark, New Jersey. Part of this money would cover initial storage there, as well as introductory exhibits at the museum. Once this was done, remaining funds would pay for rent, setting up work spaces, and preparing everything for its final move to the museum. (This took three years.) Two million dollars would be spent on the permanent exhibition. Two million would cover the purchase and installation of collection storage units, offices, equipment, and moving the machines to the museum. Five million dollars would be set aside for a restricted endowment dedicated to the care and conservation of the collection. These figures proved to be realistic and comfortably secured the acquisition project.

At the time of our Guinness negotiations, the Morris Museum had a fabulous chief financial officer. The board of trustees' fiscal oversight was dutiful. What endowment we had was conservatively invested. We always had a balanced, if lean, annual operating budget. The finance committee of the board was very well connected in the banking and investing fields (causing the aforementioned, if optimistic, loan possible). It was easy for me to make the case that the projected Guinness estate funding would be properly accounted for.

In retrospect the museum's board of trustees made one miscalculation during the planning stages for acquiring the Guinness collection. Fortunately, it did not violate the eventual gift agreement. The trustees decided to use the acquisition occasion to renovate and substantially expand the museum. This capital program included the new gallery expressly for the Guinness collection (as paid for by Guinness funding) but also a new museum entrance and other upgrades and improvements. Ten million dollars were borrowed through a New Jersey State trust fund, guaranteed by Chase Bank. I hate museum debt and have always worked to avoid it. Predictably, and well after my retirement (whew), fundraising to meet debt payments fell short and the museum renegotiated the loan. Chase obviously had no interest in foreclosing on a museum, so favorable new terms were agreed upon.

The year-end deadline for our Guinness collection proposal made the document my top executive assignment in the last two months of 2002. I wrote it over the holidays (and still owe my family a Christmas). It was not long, being about 36 pages. I discussed why the collection must be saved and in its entirety. I explained why the Morris Museum was the ideal institution to care for and promote the acquisition to the world. This included the focus on celebrating creativity in art, science, history, and theater. Our location in the metropolitan New York City region was highlighted, including ease of access by train, bus, car, and air (especially for international visitors). The quality of our board of trustees was noted. An emphasis was placed on the qualifications of our staff. Short biographies of all were included. In addition to relevant employees (whom the lawyers had met), I planned to hire a superb guest curator and exhibition design firm. Accompanying the proposal was a packet of material including annual reports, our most recent audit and 990 federal Internal Revenue Service tax documents, a staff organization chart and operating policies, and various marketing pamphlets and fliers along with the theater program.

Because of the speed required to submit the acquisition proposal and the holiday season, few people were involved in vetting the proposal packet. The board chair and the chair of the collection committee read drafts and made no changes. The document was referenced in board meeting minutes. I personally delivered the materials to the lawyer's New York City offices. Being mindful of the Guinness family's valued status as a long-term client, our plan was sent to be reviewed by pertinent members of the family in Ireland and England. Now, all the Morris Museum had to do was await a response. It came faster than anticipated. We were successful! All parties signed the gift paperwork in 2003. The museum implemented the approved proposal to the letter, and the collection, endowment, and programming accomplished what we had promised.

7 Unpacking the Baggage

The Smooth Acquisition and Transfer of the Lee L. Forman Collection of Bags

Jodi Kearns and Fran Ugalde

Without question the most unusual material acquisition discussed in this book is a huge collection of bags. Actually, the collection existed as a privately created museum that gained public stature with a relocation and ownership change.

Perhaps usually thought of as ephemeral utilitarian things, bags inundate society for all sorts of reasons. They serve many applications in their work to carry content of all sorts. The decision to acquire a private collection to establish a museum for that collection is hardly rare, but the objects in this case, to say the least, fall well outside what people might expect to identify as a museum specialty.

In July 2019, the Museum of Bags was transferred to the Institute for Human Science of Culture at the Cummings Center for the History of Psychology at the University of Akron and became the Lee L. Forman Collection of Bags. The donors even sent the storage shelves.

Collection Background

The first Museum of Bags was formed in phases between 2001 and 2003. It was dissolved in 2019 when a new home for the collection was secured.

Lee L. Forman (née Lavinthal) began collecting bags in the 1970s around the time she completed a bachelor of arts in graphic design from the American University, including the artistic bags from Bloomingdale's. Over 25 years, the collection grew to nearly 12,000 bags. Bags in this collection are both functional bags, like Bloomingdale's shopping bags, gift bags, and totes, and representative bags, such as clothing and dishes depicting bags, newspaper clippings from the funny pages with bag jokes, and upcycled bags used to produce new items, like a small area rug made from woven plastic grocery bags. The collection contains fine art, such as blown-glass sculpture and a signed Andy Warhol soup can print on a paper bag. Air sickness bags, airbags, a body bag, salt and pepper shakers, a bag signed by all four Beatles ahead of their American debut, and a Bedouin bedding bag comprise the collection. If you can imagine it, Lee L. Forman probably collected it: political bags from every presidential election since 1948, gummies and cookies, the 12-inch wooden patent model of a machine (dated 1867 – the oldest object in the collection) for making paper bags, and a paper bag that celebrities

DOI: 10.4324/9781003216384-8

including Brendan Fraser, Molly Shannon, Tina Fey, and Christopher Walken sat on that Conan O'Brien auctioned off for autism research.

Museum visitors accessed the collection primarily through a website launched in 2007 and a storage and showcase facility on the Formans' property. Built on a viable financial and organizational foundation, the museum offered educational and compelling exhibitions and programs that challenged the way visitors look at a bag.

After her death in 2009, Lee's husband Howard kept life in the collection by continuing to grow it, especially items that had long eluded the collectors and items to fill content gaps. Howard's collecting lacked Lee's zeal though it honored her mission and vision for the Museum of Bags under the tagline: *Bags as cultural icons*. The mission of the Museum of Bags was *to showcase the bag in all of its forms as an icon which illustrates the history and culture of society*. The vision of the Museum of Bags was *to be recognized as an innovative and dynamic museum noted internationally for its collection of bags*. And in 2017, Howard Forman began looking for a suitable institution to donate Lee's collection to – an organization the bags could well serve and not merely live out its days in storage.

Institutional Background

The Institute for Human Science and Culture is one of three arms that comprise the Drs. Nicholas & Dorothy Cummings Center for the History of Psychology (Cummings Center) at the University of Akron (UA), which is housed in a four-story, repurposed, and renovated historical building two blocks east of downtown Akron, Ohio. The tagline of the Cummings Center is *exploring what it means to be human*, and under this purview, the three arms offer exhibitions, collections, and space for the university and community to explore. The museum and the archives are centered on the historical record of psychology, while the institute explores other aspects of the human condition. The National Museum of Psychology is the public face of the Cummings Center's mission *to promote the history of psychology and related human sciences to the broadest community possible* and showcases objects and documents central to exploring psychology as a profession, as a science, and as an agent of social change. The Archives of the History of American Psychology (established in 1965) is the world's largest repository of manuscripts, monographs, media, and artifacts relevant to the history of psychology and related human sciences. The archives are the Cummings Center's scholarship space. The institute is a community education and gathering space consisting of state-of-the art storage facilities, 6,000+ square feet of gallery space, and a library for viewing selected off-exhibit collections. The institute is a multidisciplinary institute that promotes education and research in the history, preservation, documentation, and interpretation of the human experience through cultural objects. Prior to June 2019, the institute sported two key collections: the Oak Native American Ethnographic Collection and the David P. Campbell Postcard Collection.

Figure 7.1 Drs. Nicholas & Dorothy Cummings Center for the History of Psychology at the University of Akron

The primary activity of the Institute for Human Science and Culture is education in all its forms, including for-credit courses at the University of Akron and the country's only undergraduate certificate in museums and archives studies. Additionally, the galleries and library are spaces for designing, researching, and installing exhibitions, live events, and idea propagation within institute collections. Institute collections include cultural objects such as paintings, photographs, sculptures, ethnographic materials, films, historical and contemporary documents like books, manuscripts, films, correspondence, and sound recordings that document the human condition. The institute collection policy states that all collections considered for deposit *must have inherent educational value for University of Akron students and could also be engaging to community learners* and that

Figure 7.2 Galleries, Drs. Nicholas & Dorothy Cummings Center for the History of Psychology at the University of Akron

Figure 7.3 Students Preparing and Installing Exhibitions in the Galleries of the Drs. Nicholas & Dorothy Cummings Center for the History of Psychology at the University of Akron, Akron, Ohio

collections must have the potential to enhance learning through experiential, hands-on learning opportunities and projects. These statements also appear in the deed of gift donors sign when materials are transferred.

Cultivating a Relationship

In 2018, Howard Forman was introduced to the director of the Cummings Center, Dr. David Baker, by a colleague, learning of Forman's collection and expressing interest in it. Dr. Baker was invited to visit the Museum of Bags in Virginia, and shortly after his visit, Howard Forman and Elaine Weinstein visited the Institute for Human Science and Culture at the Cummings Center. A couple of months later, the institute director and curator visited the museum to experience the collection for themselves and to take rough measurements and photographs to determine the storage and preservation needs of the collection of bags.

The donors, the institute staff, and the university's development team agreed on the conditions of the deposit, which included all of the bags in the Museum of Bags and a significant financial gift to curate and research the collection. The donor signed a deed of gift transferring the collection to the University of Akron.

[Authors' note: It seems simple and unremarkable because cultivating a relationship with the donors was effortless. Further, what seems unremarkable in descriptions is a reflection of mutual appreciation with a common goal of preserving the Lee L. Forman Collection of Bags as cultural objects that are windows through which we peer to explore what it means to be human.]

Bags Delivered

Howard Forman hired Crozier, a fine art packing and moving company, to pack and deliver the Lee L. Forman Collection of Bags from Virginia to the Cummings Center in Akron, Ohio, in summer 2019, which consisted of two truckloads of carefully packed materials. Crozier employees packed the materials in Virginia and delivered all materials directly to the institute on the third floor of the Cummings Center.

Bags On Site

The Formans had stored nearly all of the items in the Museum of Bags in archival storage boxes, and objects not in archival storage boxes were carefully wrapped and boxed for transfer. They even sent the shelves, metadata, reference books, organizational records, and some essential equipment.

Transitioning to the Cummings Center storage, organization, and digital repository was effortless, except for time, because the collection of around 12,000 bags was almost entirely stored in archivally sound conditions, had been photographed, and had exceedingly descriptive and administrative metadata by the Formans and other Museum of Bags staff and volunteers. The Cummings Center digital project manager selected fields and uploaded the Formans' metadata directly to the CONTENTdm repository, and a student assistant inserted the photographs over a few weeks. Selections of the original metadata and all original photographs are available to search at www.uakron.edu/bags. The curator and a student assistant unpacked the boxes of bags and unwrapped bags not in boxes and sorted the delivered materials into their processed categories before giving them a new home in the storage facility.

On September 12, 2019, the Institute for Human Science and Culture held its ribbon cutting in a private ceremony commemorating construction completion and the opening of the galleries. For the opening, a student assistant who had completed her Museums & Archives Studies certificate selected and installed a sneak peek display for the opening, at which the Formans were VIP guests.

Metadata and Photographs

We cannot emphasize enough what a gift the original owners' metadata were to this collection. Usually, a curator, librarian, or archivist photographs, accessions, and creates public records for consumption. The Museum of Bags metadata is often personal and exceedingly descriptive to accounts that Cummings Center staff and students may have written under a more product/less process general practice.

Figure 7.4 Students preparing and installing exhibitions in the galleries of the Drs. Nicholas & Dorothy Cummings Center for the History of Psychology at the University of Akron, Akron, Ohio, USA

Bag, Advertising. Small brown paper bag that was originally made to hold a 45 rpm record. The bag has split on one side so now the two halves lay flat. The left half of the bag has diagonal, alternating stripes in subdued black and white with musical notes in the opposite color across the stripe. There are drawings of flat, purple vinyl records overlaying the stripes, 3 across and 3 down. The right half of the bag is brown and includes the signatures in black ballpoint pen of all 4 of the British singing group, the Beatles. At the top, Paul McCartney has handwritten "To Pat" and "love from the Beatles" Below that is a partial horizontal line with "Paul McCartney" signed below it. Below his signature on the left is "John Lennon" on the right is "George Harrison" and below those is "Ringo Starr" in the bottom left corner. Below each signature are signs of kisses, some number of "xxx"s. The bag was previously auctioned by Christie's on May 25, 2006. The founders, Lee and Howard Forman, purchased the bag from Mike Spanogiannis on July 14, 2007. (HFL2007.001.001)

Bag, Store. Brown paper bag with random darker brown lines forming a background pattern. Near the top is pasted on a 4" x 5 1/2" color painting of the

Unpacking the Baggage 95

Figure 7.5 Gallery exhibition opening, Drs. Nicholas & Dorothy Cummings Center for the History of Psychology at the University of Akron, Akron, Ohio, USA

Figure 7.6 Bag Donors With Center Staff Examining Pieces Upon Arrival of the Collection, Drs. Nicholas & Dorothy Cummings Center for the History of Psychology at the University of Akron

head and shoulders of a lovely young dark-haired woman against a gold background. In the bottom left corner of the painting is "(c) LOUIS F. DOW CO." "PUBLISHED FOR" "DEUBENER SHOPPING BAG" and "INDIANAPOLIS, IND." in tiny black lettering. Reverse has the same background pattern; no other markings. There is a single vertical seam down the center of the back. Handles are thin tightly woven paper the same color as the bag. The handles are strung all the way around the top and bottom of the bag. Side panels have the same background pattern; no other markings. The bottom of the bag has the same pattern. A brown rectangle is pasted on the bottom which is outlined in short vertical green lines. There are two small sections separated off on the left and right ends and a larger section in the center. On the left end, is a drawing of a hand holding a shopping bag with the handles around the top and bottom as on this bag. At the top is "TRADE MARK" in green lettering. On the bag is "DEUBENER'S SHOPPING BAG" "PATENTED MAY 27, 1919" and "INDIANAPOLIS, IND." in green lettering.

The complete metadata element set includes the following fields, most of which were effortlessly transferred to the Cummings Center's system without edits. Asterisked elements are available to the public in the online repository.

Figure 7.7 Bags Arrive at the Drs. Nicholas & Dorothy Cummings Center for the History of Psychology at the University of Akron, Akron, Ohio

Unpacking the Baggage 97

Figure 7.8 Storage shelving Drs. Nicholas & Dorothy Cummings Center for the History of Psychology at the University of Akron, Akron, Ohio, USA

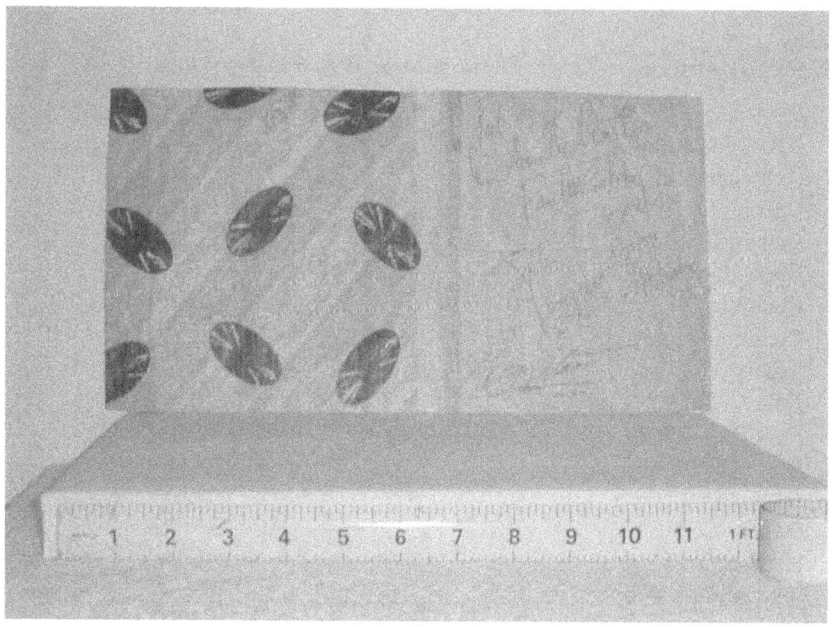

Figure 7.9 Bag, Advertising. Small brown paper bag that was originally made to hold a 45 rpm record

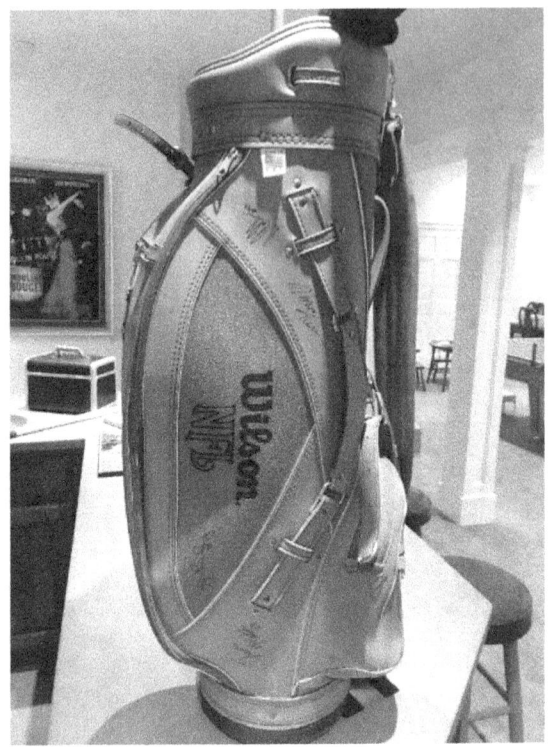

Figure 7.10 Golf bag autographed by some of the 1994 Washington Redskins

Accession Number*
Associated Name*
Catalog Entry Date
Cataloguer
Collection*
Condition
Condition Notes
Credit
Date
Depth
Description*
Diameter
Donor
Height
Image File Name*
Location
Material*
Object ID*

Collection categories were determined by Museum of Bags staff and are used as access points in the current online repository hosting the collection. They are as follows:

Advertising Bag Collection
Air Bag Collection
Air Sickness Bag Collection
Bloomingdale's Bag Collection
Book, Stationery, Envelope, Paper Collection
Brown Paper Bag Collection
Burlap Bag Collection
Ceramic Bag Collection
Cinch Bag Collection
Cloth Bag Collection
Cookie Jar Collection
Currency Bag Collection
Doll Collection
Decorative Bag Collection
Fine Arts Collection
Glass Bag Collection
Holiday Bag Collection
International Bag Collection
Jewelry Bag Collection
Key Chain Collection
Laundry Bag Collection
Leather Bag Collection
Magnet Collection
Metal Bag Collection
Miscellaneous Bag Collection
Mont Blanc Bag Collection
Museum Bag Collection
Newsprint Bag Collection
Pillow Bag Collection
Plain Bag Collection
Plastic Bag Collection
Political Bag Collection
Postal Bag Collection
Potato Bag Collection
Presidential Election Collection
Rice Bag Collection
Salt and Pepper Shaker Collection
Sports Bag Collection
Store Bag Collection
Straw Bag Collection
Tote Bag Collection
Unique Bag Collection

Vinyl Record Collection
Wine Bag Collection
Wood Bag Collection
X-Rated Bag Collection

Continuing Donations

The institute is not working to grow the Lee L. Forman Collection of Bags. Howard Forman explained that the Museum of Bags grew out of collectors and donations from all over the world and asked if we would like these donors to be directed to us. We do not. Instead, Forman has agreed to triage these donation requests, since he knows the collection better than anyone else: if Mr. Forman tells us we *need* to add a bag to the collection, we will, with him as the intermediary.

Since the original transfer in summer 2019, we have received three packages from Howard Forman. The first is Baggy Bear, which was part of the 2004 art exhibition PandaMania installed throughout Washington, D.C.: www.jophan.org/pandamania/. Baggy Bear was sponsored by the Museum of Bags and painted by artist Robert Alston with images of bags from the collection. Howard Forman tracked down the current owner, Vaughn Ripley, who donated to the institute in 2020 and sent via Crozier to join the collection in Akron.

Two additional small packages arrived a week apart in late summer 2020 from Howard Forman: one contained two face masks designed from fabric mimicking Bloomingdale's bags, and the other held two canvass bags sporting logos of the two large-party candidates for the 2020 presidential election. The latter came with the note from Howard: "You will need these to continue to say there is at least one bag from every Presidential Campaign since 1948."

Works in Progress

The mission of the institute is operationalized through education, and the first educational challenge within the Lee L. Forman Collection of Bags was given to a group of ten students working on earning their undergraduate certificates in Museums & Archives Studies: research, design, and install a full-scale museum exhibition showcasing and interpreting bags. Students selected objects that spoke to them to individually research and develop stories, and they needed to work with the team to build unifying and transitional themes to direct the flow of exhibition content. Individually, students selected themes that intersected with their personal interests: sports, politics, fine art, pop culture, food, and music, and they pulled together under the working exhibition title: *Cultural Carry-On: America's Literal Baggage*.

On March 12, I sent an email to Howard Forman and Elaine Weinstein that the students had chosen an exhibition title. And on March 12, later that day, I emailed the Formans to tell them the university would finish the spring 2020 semester with online and remote learning because of COVID-19 and safety precautions. In the end, UA policy kept staff and students offsite, and the planned exhibition was not installed.

Since the exhibition is the final project for the course, curator Fran Ugalde developed an alternative final project and had students create exhibition design documents indicating how the exhibition should be installed when it was eventually safe to do so. In the fall 2020 semester, one student who helped design the exhibit completed her Capstone Experience to earn her certificate by installing a version of the planned exhibition with the curator. Institute staff work with students and volunteers to continue work on upgrading photography, developing a full and localized inventory, and writing content to match internal policy and digging for the stories. The cultural objects of the Lee L. Forman Collection of Bags inspire a trove of educational projects, research experiences, and exhibition opportunities.

In Brief

Working with these donors is delightful and educational. We continue developing our relationship.

A Note From Howard Forman

I decided I needed to find a home for the Museum of Bags collection in 2016. Neither I nor my children were interested in furthering my late wife's passion. One of my concerns was how to maintain what I perceived was the diversity of the collection. I was certain that I might find a taker for parts of it, but not all of it. It was hard to imagine that any one institution would be able to use all of the collection, which left me wondering if I would have to break it up and what would I do if I ended up with some of it gone, but not all of it. After all, the mission of the museum was to showcase the bag in all of its forms as an icon that illustrates the history and culture of society.

I was introduced to David Baker through a mutual acquaintance. He came to see the collection on my birthday in 2018. His reaction was just what I was looking for. He said, "I get it." It was obvious that he grasped the importance and meaning of the collection.

What stood out to me about the Cummings Center, besides the bags having a place where they could be seen and researched, was the idea that the collection would be used to teach students about how to run a museum. To me, it was a win-win situation – I found a great home for the collection, and it will be used to further the original idea behind the museum. An added benefit was the friendliness of everyone we worked with during the transition.

My family and I look forward to opening of the first student-curated exhibit of bags, which will hopefully take place in May 2021.

Bibliography of News and Popular Press Articles

The intrigue of the Museum of Bags, now the Lee L. Forman Collection of Bags, has made news. The following is a short list of articles currently (to date) available online about the collection.

Barton, M.A. 2014, 'Did You Know? McLean is Home to The Museum of Bags', *Patch*, 20 May. Available from: https://patch.com/virginia/mclean/did-you-know-mclean-is-home-to-museum-of-bags.

Byard, K. 2019, 'UA Bags Quirky Collection of . . . Bags: Some 12,000 Have Been Donated', *Akron Beacon Journal*, 17 December. Available from: www.beaconjournal.com/news/20191217/ua-bags-quirky-collection-of-bags-some-12000-have-been-donated; www.pressreader.com/usa/usa-today-us-edition/20200106/281732681415167.

Kelly, J. 2014, 'In a McLean Condo, Thousands of Bags Tell the History of America', *Washington Post*, 14 May. Available from: www.washingtonpost.com/local/in-a-mclean-condo-thousands-of-bags-tell-the-history-of-america/2014/05/14/299e3d5a-db76–11e3–8009–71de85b9c527_story.html.

Rogers, P.D. 2015, 'To Collector, Shopping Bags are Art: It's a Humble Art Form, But One That Intrigues Thousands of Collectors', *News & Record*, 26 January. Available from: https://greensboro.com/to-collector-shopping-bags-are-art-its-a-humble-art-form-but-one-that-intrigues/article_9a02cce4-e681–5432-a2e1–53317b5218f1.html.

Staihar, J. 2019, 'The Museum of Bags Goes to College', *The Georgetown Dish*, 25 November. Available from: www.thegeorgetowndish.com/thedish/museum-bags-goes-college#:~:text=Forman%20Bag%20Collection%20now%20is,Museum%20and%20Archives%20Certificate%20Program.

USA Today Network 2020, 'Bounty of Bags, Parrot False Alarm, Virtual Hike: News from Around Our 50 States, (see Ohio)', *USA Today*, 6 January. Available from: www.usatoday.com/story/news/50-states/2020/01/06/bounty-bags-parrot-false-alarm-virtual-hike-news-around-states/40948393/.

Zachar, K. 2020, 'Unpacking America's Baggage', *Cummings Center Blog*, 17 April. Available from: https://centerhistorypsychology.wordpress.com/tag/lee-l-forman-bag-collection/.

8 How We Got Our F-16 Fighting Falcon

James Walther

Most museum collections fit in accessible storage, study, or, exhibition spaces and facilities. However, there are collections that present oversize challenges. Airplanes certainly fall within this category. Cars, boats, trains, building components, and big mammal skeletons are a few other examples. For some museums, large single objects can be collection exceptions or the rule. However, institutions devoted to automobiles, airplanes, and trains have obvious larger space needs. Museums with only one or a few such objects will deal with less pressing location realities.

Regardless of a museum's mission, if a sizable item is being acquired, certain unique practical demands must be addressed. This chapter provides an illuminating story about a substantial single collecting venture. The object discussed is a "retired" fighter jet owned by the U.S. military. Its acquisition tale is complicated but shows the value of perseverance.

The word connoisseur is traditionally applied to people involved with and knowledgeable about collecting the visual and decorative arts. I have long thought that sentiment unfair and certainly inapplicable in the world of museum collecting. Here we can learn about how connoisseurship plays a critical role when it comes to acquiring a fighter jet.

Muddling the acquisition process was the fact that the collecting museum was transitioning from being owned by the federal government to being a private nonprofit entity similar in operating structure to most private American charities. While the change in legal status has obvious ramifications, of equal if not more importance in this narrative is the role volunteers played in supporting the outcome of the acquisition.

As with many nonprofit organizations in the United States, volunteers are commonly invited to participate in aspects of their work. This is obvious at their governance level, since most boards of trustees are volunteers. Individuals can provide additional support in many other areas, depending on the organization. For museums volunteers can run fundraising groups, help with programming activities, donate expertise in areas of need, and generally interact with specialist or general community interests on behalf of the museum. The story of the acquisition of the fighter jet relies almost totally on the sweat equity and goodwill of a loyal corps of volunteers.

DOI: 10.4324/9781003216384-9

In about 1997, two F-16 aircraft built for the U.S. Air Force by Lockheed Martin Corp. were abandoned by the Air Force at Kirtland Air Force Base in Albuquerque, New Mexico. They were to be used by the Department of Energy's research lab there. Known as Sandia National Labs, it is a large multimission engineering laboratory that performs design and testing functions in support of the U.S. Nuclear Weapons Defense Program. By this time, however, the Cold War was over and the number of jets needed to defend the United States from attack by the former Soviet Union had ceased with the collapse of the USSR in 1991. These two aircraft were in reasonable condition back then and were being held for physical destructive testing purposes if needed. That means that the laboratory could use them to test the hardness of defensive structures made of concrete or other materials to help determine how vulnerable the structures might be in case of future attack. One of the F-16s was in more complete condition than the other, but both were left on federal property for this use. While this plan and condition had been the case back in 1997, by 2014, they had deteriorated considerably, as these two planes had not been used for their intended purpose. During all the years of the F-16 use, more than 1,000 were built for our defense.

When I, as director of the National Museum of Nuclear Science & History, which is near the location of the two jets, heard about them, I immediately wanted to acquire one for its collections. This was before the September 11, 2001, attacks on the World Trade Center towers. This event heighted interest in U.S. air defense but had no impact on the destiny of these planes. At the time I started looking into acquiring one or both, the National Atomic Museum (predecessor to the current National Museum of Nuclear Science & History) was also located at Kirtland Air Force Base in Albuquerque. Upon inspecting the aircraft in their rather forlorn location in the desert on base lands, I immediately decided to seek ownership. My first challenge was to find a place for them at the museum, which had several static airplanes adjacent but not yet a place to add another one. However, I needed to figure out who owned them and how they could become the museum's. The aircraft had been where we saw them for so long, but no record of their original acceptance by any agency could be found and thus no ownership was easily confirmed.

Officials at the Sandia laboratories wanted to rid the area of these old objects, but they presented technical difficulty if they wanted to merely destroy them. The destruction posed environmental concerns that could end up being costly to undertake, which explained why they had rested undisturbed in the bright, hot New Mexico sun for 17 years.

Our federal government is very careful to establish ownership of something as theirs before they can do something like disassemble or move it. The planes were definitely federal property, but which branch could claim them? Were they still Air Force property? Not really, as they had been dropped from active force roles when they were abandoned. There was a record of that, but no record of them being transferred to the Department of Energy. Yet they were on that department's property and under the care of its laboratory. Sandia was in "possession" and seemed to be responsible but could not prove ownership. There was information available about the jets' value from the federal government. They cost taxpayers about $14.6 million back in the late 1970s when new. (In present dollars that would have been just over $30 million each.) As scrap they were valued by weight at about $4,000 each. Thus any financial interest was absent regarding their destiny. It was clear the Air Force had no use or interest in these objects. They were too old to fly, and they were not needed for their original testing applications.

The question for me was: How to get these planes? Some background on the museum will be helpful regarding the unusual circumstances I was dealing with when it came to collecting. To understand how the location of old aircraft on the air base was an opportunity requires an explanation of the operations and history of this unique museum. There are nuances uncommon elsewhere in the museum field.

The museum is found in public law and is chartered by the Congress as America's Museum Resource for Nuclear Science & History. The mission is broad and covers military as well as peaceful applications of atomic energy be they for medicine, industry, or power generation, to name a few. While the language established the museum as a federal agency, at the time we sought the jets, it was transitioning from direct operations by the Department of the Environment and its laboratory on the Air Force base to a private nonprofit organization. And that nonprofit was planning to create a new purpose-built museum building that it would operate independently from the government at a much-reduced cost. Complicating this plan happened was the 9/11 attacks, as the Air Force base was closed to the general public. The museum was forced to move to remain in service, first to a temporary rented facility and finally to the brand-new place near, but not on, the base.

The museum, now operated as a not-for-profit entity governed by a board of directors, undertook a capital campaign to construct a large new facility on 12 acres of land provided to it by the Department of the Environment. Since the department remained legally obligated to have the museum but did not want to pay it for it, providing its land was seen as an easy way of supporting this ownership obligation.

The museum therefore exists upon federal property and has a very nominal land-lease agreement in perpetuity. This arrangement allows easy placement of federal property for display at the museum. And it allows a continuing program to acquire federal assets for preservation and display. This, of course, made acquiring the jets an easy possibility.

Having explained the nature of the National Museum of Nuclear Science & History, I will now turn to its collections, which, obviously, is why we wanted one or both of the airplanes under discussion. Because the museum holds a federal/national charter established in public law but also operates as a nonprofit entity it has two distinct collections.

The collection that existed when the nonprofit organization was established is totally federal property. This traces to 1969 when the museum began. These materials do not comprise a very large body of objects consisting primarily of really big things like a B-52 fighter plane, a B-29 fighter plane, a Minuteman I Missile, and the largest unclassified group of nuclear weapons in the world that can be viewed by the public. There are 134 of these objects. Our supervision sets certain specific requirements of care and recordkeeping that are slightly different from the other collection group. This second museum collection is five times larger than the one described earlier. It is not owned by the government, having been acquired via the museum's nonprofit status. Both collections are held in the public trust, and both are administrated by a competent staff, including curatorial oversight, collections management, and registrar professionals. The museum is accredited by the American Alliance of Museums. It collects for each of its two acquisition groups. Aircraft come into the federal collections, and private objects like nuclear medical devices and cultural objects fall into the private holdings. Having decided that the museum only wanted one of the two planes, we had been determining how and where to show it and, more importantly, what condition to restore it to. The plane we wanted was in better, if also deteriorated, condition than the less preferable one. What follows is a description of these planes and why they are of such importance both militarily and locally.

The F-16 we wanted had a tail number of 78–0050 (this is painted on the aircraft). We hoped to put it on view in Heritage Park, our nine-acre display area behind the museum itself, with the other six aircraft presently shown. To achieve this goal, we planned to recondition it using a volunteer workforce and to repaint it to depict the paint scheme of the New Mexico Air National Guard. (NMANG). There is deep pride in the local community for the work of this wing of the National Guard.

The NMANG is called the "Tacos." It is an endearing moniker that has existed for more than 70 years of flying aircraft as a wing of the National Guard in New Mexico. But that wing, which flew a strong group of F-16s, was decommissioned from Albuquerque in 2006. Its jets were transferred to another state Air National Guard. Our group was assigned a new and different mission. Thus, there was interest in placing a representative F-16 on display somewhere in Albuquerque where the public could see it, walk around it, show it to kids and grandkids, and be proud of the contribution that it represented in defense of our nation. No other F-16 airplane displays were in the region. My plan was to make this F-16 that object of pride and memory for our citizens – if I could get it.

The particular F-16 I wanted is an early one. These planes were built in "blocks" of 10 at a time, and this was #50. Being from block #50, as the tail number indicated, we knew it dated to 1978. It has some unique materials for its time, including carbon-fiber rear horizontal stabilizers and other cutting-edge, for its era, avionics. Its overall condition would be described as "poor" when we began consideration. But it was by no means a lost cause. And since another just like it but in even worse condition was also out in the desert sitting next to #50, a chance to cannibalize that jet was an option to bring #50 back to full trim. Most of the parts were still on this jet, except the gunnery and some details of canopy cover. It was missing rivets in places because it had served as a way to test making field repairs, so patches and malformed metal places were evident. It still had its engine and most trim pieces. The landing gear was intact, and it serviceable tires. It seemed to have had its "explosive bolts" and ejection seat drives removed. This is really important, as these technologies can be dangerous if not disabled properly by Air Force mechanics. You are required to create and maintain a record that this removal was completed and properly. Fortunately the plane had no fuel after sitting outside for 17 years, but some of the hydraulic systems inside the jet held fluids still. There was a bit of history mystery. We found out that the New Mexico Guard is one of a few state guard units authorized to transport a nuclear weapon. This is due to the location of two large weapons laboratories and three Air Force bases located inside the state. I guess if an emergency or a war broke out, our planes would have moved these defense materials safely if required.

By about 2012, the Department of the Environment laboratory professionals were trying to assist me in physically getting the jet. They too wanted it gone. It represented a piece of old junk that was taking up valuable space, had potential environmental issues, and was still on their inventory listings as abandoned. As much as they wanted to help, however, no one could figure out the plane's ownership in any definitive way. (It was nine miles from the museum, at the south end of Kirtland Air Force base on land used by the national laboratory, not the Air Force.) For us it was a case of so far and yet so close.

Because my plan was to move this plane intact in one piece to the museum and paint it as a tribute to the NMANG, I felt it was a perfect opportunity to garner

Figure 8.1 Moving the F-16 on a bright Sunday in May 2014. The maximum speed was 5 mph for the old tires, and the trip between the abandoned site and museum was nine miles. Volunteers drove the truck using a borrowed Air Force regulation tow bar. (Photo: Major Jerry Hanks USMC, retired)

high-profile publicity and gin up enthusiastic community support for both the National Guard and the museum by asking the National Guard leaders to help with the move to the museum. Initially all went well after meeting with several Air Force colonels and commanders, who concurred that it was a wonderful way to show spirit and community pride in our work. It looked rosy for a while. The National Guard could get the proper tow bar, it had access to the Air Force base, it could inspect the aircraft to ensure a safe move, and it had the "tug" to pull the thing. All appeared to be a "go." But as often happens, the legal side of things saw the liability in these efforts as too great. Military lawyers decided that since there was no established true owner, neither the Air Force nor Department of the Environment could touch or move it. Needless to say, after my high hopes I was extremely disappointed by this decision. It set my plans back by six months at least. I immediately looked for other ways to proceed.

While searching for alternative options to move the plane, back at the museum we had prepared a spot to display it. It would be placed with four other fighter aircraft, all nuclear weapon–capable carriers, in the south end of Heritage Park. We measured carefully the space available so it wouldn't be too close to the others and would leave room for additional planes collected in the future, as well as provide a clear space to tow it on to the site.

The F-16 is about 36 feet wide from wingtip to wingtip. We were not planning to take the wings off, as it is a difficult, if not impossible, task and we don't have the skill or equipment to do so anyway. Large airplanes like our B-52 required us to hire specialty companies that could dismantle parts of these planes to move them on big flat-bed trailers. But this plane was to be towed as a unit. The entry gate to the museum area was too narrow. We therefore converted our south chain-link fenced gate. A fence company was hired to make the fence slide to accommodate the full 36-foot wingspan, which was just barely wide enough to pull it through.

We always put our aircraft on concrete pads, poured to a proper depth to support the weight of the plane. The F-16 is pretty light, at only about nine tons, so the pads could be simple. Nevertheless, determining their size and spacing was critical. By this time we had a loyal group of volunteers helping with the project. They dug holes and poured the concrete. The ground here is a type of "caliche" that is almost as hard as concrete, so we use a jack-hammer to break it up when needed. In fact, the museum has its own jack-hammer just for this purpose.

Towing an airplane requires a specialized tow bar, which is attached to a truck, tractor, or other powerful vehicle. The bar is configured for specific airplane applications. The museum does not own any tow bars, since we don't move planes around as a rule. We had to find one, which we did and borrowed it for the job.

An obviously critical challenge with moving the plane was establishing a safe and convenient towing transit route. We would need to be allowed and able to have the proper clearance to pull a plane that is 36 feet wide down the streets or roadways without taking out road signs or low-hanging power lines or disrupting traffic. The tail of this jet is 22 feet tall, so it can snag a power line hanging across a roadway.

The F-16 was in the desert on a dirt road, inside what is called a "technical area." This is an access-restricted space where you must have a certain authorization, denoted with a specific badge, to be there due to other work conducted in the area. As a national security space, getting the proper access credentials for volunteers and staff can take some time and involve being escorted when in the area itself. Because driving in and out of a tech area is controlled by gates and security arms, there is no way to get something like a big wide jet through them. We had to see if other nonregular vehicle routes with bigger gates were evident along the perimeter of the fences. We found one. It looked like the plane would just squeeze through so we could get it outside the security area, but only if we could find the right authorities with the right keys to the locks to open for us on our desired move date. The plane needed to be towed through that big gate to a larger two-lane road, which was at least paved even if still on the base. Kirtland Air Force Base is huge, as some western military reservations are. It encompasses thousands of acres. Pulling the jet off the base would mean driving it through the base housing areas as it headed to the city and the museum site.

As 2014 dawned, I was deciding that we could not use the initial crew promised us. Military brass feared liability issues in assisting us. They had initially proposed this idea as a training activity so that military personnel could try their hand at moving a jet. I began to talk to a long-term partner that the museum has, a construction company whose headquarters building is across the street. Since we now had borrowed a tow bar to fit the plane, what we needed next was a really big truck capable of towing its weight, as well as a qualified person to drive it. Our good friends at J.B. Henderson Construction came through for us and offered to provide a tractor cab and driver.

Before the plane could be moved from its site, I was told I must complete and have assessed the environmental impact of its move. There is a federal law, the National Environmental Protection Act (NEPA) of Congress, that governs most disturbances and work done on federal property. Digging, moving, placing, and building all have impacts that can be detrimental, so an assessment of impact is performed. It is called a NEPA Checklist, and it can take time to do it properly and get it approved. I started on it as soon as I was told it would be required. For example, I had to assure the plane would not leak fluids while being moved, that it would not be an impediment to traffic, and that no birds were nesting in it. This sort of bureaucracy can take a while to process, so it was important to submit the information as soon as possible. It was given to the National Laboratory. As the submission entered their system, it resulted in a "you want to do what?" response. After explaining my plan to simply move the object, they settled down to help me understand any compliance considerations we would have to deal with.

The F-16 had three tires, one up front and two mounted on struts on each wing. It is a common way for aircraft landing gear to be engineered. The tires on the airplane had been sitting out in the sun for 20 years and were in poor condition. Strangely the ones on the other less complete airplane were in better condition. It looked like we might want to swap out the bad tires on our plane for better ones on the sister unit. We had never taken a tire off of an F-16 jet fighter, and believe me, it is no simple task. First, the airplane is a lot heavier than even a pretty large truck, and the jacking points are a bit strange. Without access to the proper Air Force equipment needed to lift an F-16, we improvised. We actually Googled "Removing a tire from an F-16" and watched several YouTube videos to understand what the process called for. It was very helpful. For instance we knew we were going to "foam" the wheels. The foaming injects a semi-rigid polyurethane foam inside the tire tubes instead of air pressure. This means we needed to swap tires and take them to a specialty tire shop in the city for this. It works well as long as the craft is mostly static, which this was to be after we moved it. I called the tire store that advertised this service and explained that we wanted to bring in three tires from and for an F-16 fighter jet. The lady on the phone had a hard time with the number thinking I meant a Ford F-150 pickup truck, therefore why only three wheels? Once we straightened everything out, we took the tires to the company for injecting. The product cures for 24 hours. We were then back in the desert where we could jack the plane up and get the tires on it. There was a catch, though; the maximum speed to roll the tires is 10 mph. To be conservative for the higher weight, I set a limit of 5 mph. Calculating a travel distance of nine miles at 5 mph would make for a long morning, with many stops for traffic.

At this point in the acquisition process, the only way the museum could move the aircraft was to rely on our great partners and volunteers. Our devoted friends had often helped us with industrial equipment such cranes, backhoes, front-end loaders, or big forklifts. It has saved us a lot of money over the years. We were thrilled that J.B. Henderson Construction Co. donated the use of a huge truck to hitch the tow bar to pull the jet. What a relief to secure this. Now we could count on the right-sized equipment to assist us. We had tried it with a pickup truck, but no way would the plane move more than a few feet. I was sure we were going to blow a transmission with this option.

The day we set to move the plane turned out to be for an early warm spring morning in March. The Air Force base police were notified, and we assembled our volunteers. We had on orange vests and hard hats and walkie-talkies in hand as we met at the site. The first part of the challenge was getting the jet out of the technical area. Once we passed those gates, we moved smoothly, if very slowly. The big truck mostly idled as it maintained the - mph crawl. Moving out of the far reaches of the Air Force base and into its center areas, we came to spots where wires were too low for the tail of the jet to pass without snagging. I had scoped out a different route that avoided this even though it meant pulling the jet through the base housing areas. The whole escapade was a fun Sunday morning treat for kids and their families as we cruised their neighborhood with a big silver jet fighter in tow. There was a lot of waving and laughter and picture-taking of our convoy of trucks carrying museum volunteers and staff, with the police escort out in front.

We pulled the fighter to a spot near to the perimeter fence of the Air Force base that is right behind the museum. (The museum is beside the base but is not part of it.) Once in place we left the F-16 there overnight, still attached to the big truck. I had made signs to tape on the truck cab doors and on the side of the airplane that informed the Air Force patrols that the plane was authorized to be parked there and not to freak out (my term for a reaction of finding a fighter jet pointed at the fence from the inside).

The next morning was another beautiful spring day. I had requested base security professionals to assist a contractor to take down this fence section so the jet could be brought onto museum property. This required armed security to stand watch, as the perimeter was going to be briefly breached. It had been done before when we moved to the museum and moved several big artifacts to the new museum site. The section of fence was dismantled and rolled up temporarily. We started the tractor cab, let it warm up, then pulled the aircraft onto our back-access driveway. The fence was quickly replaced so security was re-established for the Air Force base.

We then towed the jet past the front of the museum, through the parking lots and through the gate we had expanded to fit the plane's wingspan. There were inches to spare on each side. Having successfully threaded this needle, our awesome volunteer driver then slowly backed the plane into the spot we had prepared and precisely onto the three concrete pads recently put in place to receive their load. Needless to say everyone breathed a sigh of relief. We proudly, and with great relief, stood back to admire our effort. Newspaper and television crews were there.

We received great press and lots of public interest for our plan to preserve the aircraft as a testament to the service of the men and women of the NMANG.

The plane survived the move very well, even held up. (I had nightmares about them failing in the middle of the road blocking traffic but my fears were unfounded. Whew!) We began to restore the jet to the visual specifications outlined when we were acquiring it. Again, volunteers were essential. We had a large number of aviation maintenance students from the local community college ready to assist and, of course, our own teams of volunteers. Everyone was chomping at the bit to get to work. The tasks occupied most of the rest of 2014, ending in November.

We had calculated we would need about $35,000 for the airplane acquisition project. To raise this we employed a multifaceted approach that solicited gifts at all levels. We appealed to former Air Force and Air Guard members, and many responded. Several major gifts came in to recognize the bravery and service of our national defense members. We did our first crowd-funding, which became a standard successful practice for all the airplanes we display. We, of course, held several individual fundraising and project awareness events.

Our fundraising ventures morphed into regular programming once the jet was in place and safe to work with. We began a program we call "Movie Under the Wings," which now happens mid-summer. It is an outside screening of films for the entire family, projected on the back of the museum building. We have live music, fun activities for kids, and food trucks. A brewery partner features "Bombs Away Beer." We sell about 600 tickets at $15 each. Members get $5 off. Our first movie was, appropriately, the aviation film *Top Gun*. There were $20 photo opportunities for attendees to sit in the cockpit after climbing actual air ramp ladders. The first movie event helped push us over our fundraising goal. The interest raised set the groundwork for our next fundraising project, which is the restoration of our B-29 bomber.

The dedication of the completed F-16 project was a huge success. Members attended in abundance, as well as outside donors. There were many airplane buffs, veterans, and military leaders from the National Guard and the Air Force. Our two U.S. senators and governor were there in addition to the commander of the New Mexico National Guard. Brief speeches during the ribbon-cutting focused on the important history and mission of the NMANG. The media was well-represented. The acquisition was and remains a great way to thank the NMANG and those who helped us achieve success.

9 Community Collecting Conversations

Acquisition Stories, District Museum, Jorhat, India

Abantika Parashar

For art and history museums, collecting can be a highly nuanced mating dance or an encounter quickly consummated. To be sure, success is not always guaranteed. (In fact, another book could be written about failed collecting attempts.) Convincing people to engage with a museum regarding acquisitions is often a process of persuasive cultivation. It requires mission conviction and the ability to convey that. This chapter offers insights about community collecting on a broad scale.

> "Collections are what make museum, unique. Museum collections are more than objects, they are carefully chosen assemblages, the product of a curatorial way of knowing." 'Museum needs collections and connections'[1] Steven Lubar (https://lubar.medium.com/museums-need-collections-and-connections-375543f9d331).

I am from Assam, a northeastern state of the Indian subcontinent. The museum I work for is the District Museum, Jorhat. It is a small museum, which comes under the state government administration and also serves as a district headquarters for a cluster of other districts. At present, it has almost 3,000 artifacts. They include such things as coins, manuscripts, textiles, archaeological remains, arms and armor, and everyday objects. My association with the museum as the museum officer started in 2018. This time has been a most amazing learning experience for me as a curator. I shall share my work through this chapter.

District Museum, Jorhat was established in 1989 in Jorhat District under the aegis of the state government. The mission is to collect, preserve, display, and generate an awareness among the people about their local material heritage. It is important to describe the home district, Jorhat. It is one of the major cities of Assam and a doorway to the state as well as another northeastern state, Nagaland. Jorhat was the last capital of the Ahoms, the major ruling dynasty of undivided Assam, before the advent of colonial rule, which allowed it to grow as a planned fortified town under the royal patronage. Many tanks or ponds were also built around the capital city by the Ahom royalty, apart from forts, roads, Moidams (burial sites), etc. During that time, it was a flourishing and commercial metropolis. It was eventually destroyed by a series of Burmese invasions between 1817 and 1824. Later the district was declared an administration headquarters under the

DOI: 10.4324/9781003216384-10

Figure 9.1 District Museum, Jorhat, Assam

British rule. In 1983 it was declared an independent district. The cultural diversity that has prevailed in the city for centuries has inspired the people to participate in wide-ranging cultural activities through the decades. Consequently Jorhat has produced many creative writers, musicians, actors, historians, and journalists, defining Jorhat as the cultural capital of the state.

The collection that we have today in the District Museum, Jorhat represents the ethnographic and cultural diversity of the region, as well as neighboring districts. Pristine motifs, weaving patterns, and materials of the collected textiles provide a glimpse into the colorful world and richness of the living textile tradition, whereas arms and armor, ethnographic collections, and everyday objects vividly represent the fine skills and technological advancements of a time long gone. On the other hand, the archaeological findings provide a representative history of local human past. Equally important are the silver and copper coins, manuscripts, masks, pottery, etc., which attract visitors because of their uniqueness, rarity, and heritage value.

The majority of collections have entered the museum through donations; very few are purchased. However, a certain number of artifacts have also been acquired through field acquisition. This is mostly done in case of archaeological remains, including sculptures, terracotta and coins, arms and armor, pottery, and more. In the case of such field acquisitions, we try to follow some basic guidelines. These very often unfold through memorable encounters with those who temporarily possess these items. This process results in important and fascinating collection stories. This information is of critical importance, as they inform an object's journey from discovery in the earth to the museum, making documentation complete. From my point of view, apart from organizing regular exhibitions and outreach programs, it is equally important to share the acquisition stories of the museum professionals. These narratives recognize and pay tribute to the labor, dedication, and hard work of extraordinary museum professionals, without whom museums cannot exist.

I have been permitted to conduct independent field acquisitions for three years. Though my experience was initially somewhat limited, the overall acquisition scenarios have improved substantially. This is due to the wide-ranging heritage awareness programs conducted by museums and like-minded organizations here. Unlike a few decades ago, people are now much more aware of the importance of safeguarding heritage material. This includes guarding against losses incurred when artifacts are sold in the black market. Initially, when museum personnel sought significant collections, there were even instances of resident hostility. Such reactions mostly reflected superstations, as well as ignorance of the museum activity being conducted. Today, although such unpleasantness has not totally disappeared, we collectors have to struggle less than once was the case.

I will now describe three significant and not atypical collection stories. I was more involved with two of the examples, while another person concerned was a very senior curator, who later retired from the position of director of the state archeology department. The stories are intentionally spread over a period of two decades so readers can have an overview of how acquisition work has changed from the challenges it once entailed.

But first let me answer a few questions that I very often encounter as a curator. Do you collect each and every thing when excavating or otherwise seeking items for the museum? Do you confiscate any artifacts that have heritage value but have been held by a family for a very long time? How do you get information about antiquities? Is there any law for acquisitions? The following information summarizes answers to these questions:

1. No, we do not acquire each and every thing that we find or are informed of. Before an acquisition happens, a thorough study is done about the artifacts being considered. The very first concern is: Does it have any relevance to my museum or it should be transferred to some other museum, where it has more

contextual value? This information is given top priority. The museum's space is limited, which presents challenges, as the collection is always increasing. Sometimes it even becomes a headache to accommodate artifacts in storage or in a reserved collection because of their size or fragility. Therefore, in order to avoid unnecessary difficulties, our focus must concentrate on the acquisition of artifacts specifically relevant to the aim and objectives of the museum. In our case, we try to acquire artifacts related to the tangible and intangible history of the home district, as well neighboring districts.

Things falling outside our purview are transferred either to other working agencies or to the headquarters, where objects are then dispersed to other museums as loans or donations.

2. My museum doesn't confiscate any family heirloom until and unless they are extremely rare and of high heritage value. However, in such cases we encourage the families to formally register the objects along with necessary preventive measures to ensure security, longevity, and research. The item(s) thus remain with the owners.
3. For collection-related information, we mostly depend on print, visual, and social media. We also rely on information provided by local heritage enthusiasts. The second source is the more reliable of these two. It provides basic intrinsic information that goes beyond a simple notation of its whereabouts.
4. Because my museum comes under the government of Assam, which is under the government of India, we adhere to The Antiquities and Art Treasure Act, 1972 for acquisition guidance and protocols. It has been amended several times since first being created (https://legislative.gov.in/sites/default/files/A1972-52.pdf)

In cases of field acquisitions, my museum works in collaboration with district government administrations and police departments. Because of previous instances of hostility encountered during collection activities, we museum professionals prefer to have complete police protection to ensure the security of our team. Such a team mostly includes at least a curator, one museum assistant, and one or two media professionals, followed by police personnel and sometimes representatives of a local district civil administration. We include media professionals because they can play a valuable role as high-profile catalysts to generate awareness of our work. And their presence helps confirm the authenticity about our intention in the public mind.

What follows are examples of the field acquisition work of the District Museum, Jorhat.

Kachamari Pathar, Golaghat

In the early 1990s curator Dr. Hemendra Nath Dutta with the assistance of Sh. Nikunja Singh, of the local police force, investigated what they thought might be an important finding just accidentally unearthed by a local resident. It was discovered at a site well-known to archaeologists because of several rare and priceless artifacts previously found there. The item was a rare piece of sculpture. The resident had been strictly instructed by the village leaders keep the matter quiet. Now in those days, it was very common for a superstitious Assamese village to believe such discoveries to be a divine finding. Transferring the item to a museum was regarded as a bad omen for the entire village. Instead, the inhabitants preferred to construct a temple, since in their opinion anything and everything found beneath the soil, by hook or by crook, was linked to divinity. In the case of this sculpture, however, somehow the news of it got out and eventually reached the curator.

On the day when Dr. Dutta learned about the finding, it was almost noon. Being aware of the importance of the site but mindful of the chaos that the public could create, he moved quickly to acquire the piece. With evening fast approaching, he arrived at the site. As expected, people already there were in a hostile frame of mind once they learned of the curator's intention. In declining to recognize any larger heritage value of the object, they also were not at all ready to accept the museum team's plan. They firmly believed there were evil intentions behind the acquisition desire. They started threatening the team. Some of the elderly villagers even tried to convince the museum representatives that the appearance of the sculpture was a divine signal from God. Any offensive tampering with this would lead to deadly consequences, for which the museum team would be solely responsible. The situation thus became tense. By this time the museum team, consisting of three people, faced an angry crowd of hundreds. Fortunately, a timely intervention by the police brought the situation under control. The team returned to the museum at three o'clock in the morning with the sculpture. But the collecting tale did not end there.

A few days later Dr. Dutta was informed in the early morning that more than 100 people had gathered around the museum. They loudly demanded the museum's entry gate be opened for them. He found this very strange. No visitors had ever demanded the museum to be opened and so early. He quickly went to the museum, where he learned the folks were villagers from Kachamari. They had come to verify whether "their" sculpture was actually in the museum as promised. Or had it been sold to someone? The museum staff was unprepared to handle the emotional crowd, and there was no time to ask for additional security should unexpected vandalism happen.

Dr. Dutta handled the situation very cleverly. He was aware of the fact that a polite and respectful gesture from the museum team was the only possible way to calm the angry crowd and convince them of the museum's honesty in acquiring the sculpture for public benefit, rather than some secrete private gain. Though shaking inside, with pleasant words and a smile, he talked to the crowd, assuring them of the museum's retentive interest in the sculpture and its proper physical care. He then invited people to see the piece, one by one, where the sculpture was kept. He also distributed museum literature and pamphlets and quoted several villages who had freely and even enthusiastically donated objects to museums. These included some of the crowd's neighboring areas. His words and gestures had such a magical effect that the group not only publicly apologized for its behavior but also promised to donate other things to the museum if found in their locality and worth acquiring.

The village kept its word. A major part of the archaeological collection of the District Museum, Jorhat has come from this area. Defusing the potentially eruptive confrontation between my museum's staff and the authorities supporting it had a very positive impact for the history of my museum. If handled poorly, it could have led to serious damage. The quick and mindful thinking of the curator not only saved the sculpture and the institution but also broke the ice between the public and the museum, which is very important for the success of a museum.

Mahuramukh, Golaghat

The first museum acquisition of my career was exceptional, and I look back on the experience with no little nostalgia. It came to our attention that eight spears had been found in the backyard of a family while digging for planting season. My knowledge of these and related items then was completely theoretical. I was very nervous when starting our journey to Mahuramukh. It was an almost two-hour ride from our museum. Two junior collogues were with me. Upon reaching town we checked in at the nearest police station to ask for someone to accompany us in our local venture. No one was available because of other commitments. Not wanting to return to our home, we proceeded without police assistance. However, outside the police station we were joined by two local representatives with whom we had been corresponding for the past two weeks regarding the subject of our quest.

When we reached the home of the spear discoverers, we were given a very warm welcome. The family was quite hospitable though of humble financial means. We were served beverages and light snacks, and they showed us the spears and the spot where they were unearthed. They also expressed gratitude to the museum for its wish to acquire the objects. They believed the new ownership would be the only opportunity to assure their family's public legacy in perpetuity.

After we finalized the spear gift formalities and we prepared to leave the home, we were confronted with something totally unexpected. Out of nowhere a group of approximately ten people had assembled outside the house to forbid the family to hand over the spears. We were informed that the demands were being made by what was described as "the unofficial hooligans of the village." These individuals were known for their illegal activities. Some had clearly been drinking. I soon learned that artifacts found in the area in the past had also been forcefully taken by these miscreants, the whereabouts of which are still unknown.

What had been a very pleasant situation suddenly became scary. Evidence of the seriousness of the confrontation was quickly apparent when the two local representatives quietly disappeared. For our personal safety, we carefully departed and without the objects. We still didn't have police protection that day.

We pretty much lost hope for acquiring the spears when one day I received an unexpected call. It was from the very family who had unearthed them. The person on the phone told me they now wanted to get rid of the spears because they believed them to be haunted. The family was terrified and urged us to come as soon as possible. What caused them to assume the spears were a spiritual threat was and remains unknown to me, but their feelings were fortunate for us. The next week we returned to the home and quietly acquired the spears for the District Museum, Jorhat. No local opponents were in evidence, and none have surfaced since then. The authorities support the museum's ownership.

I am still in a bit of a dilemma regarding my actions about this acquisition at the time it took place. Should I have tried to spiritually expunge the haunting of the spears and, if so, how? The sympathetic person in me says yes. At the same time the museologist inside reminds me that what I have done met the profession's demands of the situation. The donor family will definitely get a second opportunity to rectify their concerns, but I would have never had another opportunity to save those spears, which represent our heritage.

I have to confess that the museologist inside me always wins.

Dadhara, Lakshimpur

This museum collecting story is very recent and took place when I had to go for a field acquisition amidst the COVID-19 pandemic. We received news that two teenagers had found a hoard of coins and silver jewelry while fishing. They were in their possession. We knew all too well that a black market for such things is very active in that area. People very often sell artifacts for very little. Although the location is almost 300 kilometers from my museum, I immediately rushed to get the items.

Upon arrival with my team, we encountered some resistance on the part of family members. There were 15 coins, 2 of which were quite rare. One member of the family actually tried to conceal a few. With police assistance, we succeeded in recovering everything. We then carried out the necessary ownership transfer formalities. Suddenly something unexpected happened for which we were not prepared at all.

While my team was busy with arranging the official paperwork, almost the entire village had gathered in the courtyard of the house. In their presence, along with the media, when the senior-most lady of the family was handing me the sealed packet of the artifacts along with some ritualistic gestures, she started sobbing. This gradually turned into audible cries followed by others, and suddenly I discovered myself in front of a howling crowd of almost 60 as the media filmed us directly.

Today when I recall this incident, I do so with sympathetic hindsight. But then, it had made me so uncomfortable I could not think of any way to assuage or otherwise control the crowd. Even though the process and outcome of the acquisition was my responsibility, it was not possible for me to console each individual personally. To make matters more difficult, because of the deadly coronavirus, I had to maintain mandatory physical distancing. To further amplify the unusual circumstances of the event, everything was happening on camera. This meant a direct telecast in video format, which in time was actually broadcast. Of course by this time there was a police presence. Officers tried to calm the crowd, but their intercession had the opposite effect and attracted more passersby. I remained patient and hopeful as I waited for things to normalize. Fortunately the villagers consoled themselves in a timely manner. They understood the impact and importance of the acquisition and the role the museum played for them. I was able to return with these valued materials, which are deeply appreciated by the District Museum, Jorhat.

I do admit that professionally I am still an infant in the museum field and I have a long way to go. But what I feel is that apart from knowledge, public relation skills and a quick mind are the two most important assets for field acquisition. The slightest delay in making a decision or a single unexpected gesture can change a completely favorable situation, which is not only life- threatening but also at the same time a loss of our heritage. Besides, there is an unimaginable difference between theory and practicality, expectations and reality. So this is something which should be a mandatory part of museum training programs, but unfortunately is often ignored. Even in countries like India, where tradition and superstitions play a very important role in everyday life in the remote pockets, people do not have any problem in donating to museums, but their ignorance and simplicity require a different type of approach and handling. A smile or casual small talk can do wonders in such cases, for which museum professionals should be prepared beforehand. And this is how we museum professionals collect for our museums here.

Note

1 Steven Lubar (https://lubar.medium.com/museums-need-collections-and-connections-375543f9d331).

10 Collecting Nonverbal History Documents

Steven Miller

I have only worked in regional history museums. There have been six over the years, ranging from large and complex urban organizations to a single historic house. Five were private nonprofit entities, while one was a state agency. My museum preferences were probably rooted in my upbringing. Grandparents on both my father's and mother's side never threw anything out. When something was deemed of no immediate use, it was relegated to the attic of houses they had lived in just about all their lives. As a kid I reveled in exploring these. I especially remember discovering a large wooden barrel containing an ancestor's Civil War musket and equipment. My families were middle class and not wealthy, but their American experience certainly reflected pieces of our national story. My father's mother played piano in silent movie houses and then percussion with an all-female jazz band in the 1910s. Her fourth and last husband was an immigrant from Brazil who performed in vaudeville. They established a stage act in the 1920s. With the onset of the Great Depression, the theater career ended. But her drums, xylophone, and props were carefully put away in her attic, ready to come out for use (which happened when I took up drums in high school). My mother's father had been a mid-level bank clerk. He had a roll-top desk from his clerking days and pieces of beautiful nineteenth-century household furniture his grandparents had bought before they lost what would have been his comfortable inheritance to a long-gone nefarious business partner. These were all kept in his attic.

As my personal discoveries as a kid illustrate, objects can connect us to places, people, and events long gone (or in the case of contemporary collecting, quite current). The question is what should be collected? These are difficult decisions to make. However, they are made easier if we look at three-dimensional evidence in the same way we look at two-dimensional materials. Objects can be no different than paper-based records insofar as their potential informational value is concerned.

The acquisition stories I relate in this chapter describe a tiny fraction of what I have brought into museums over the years. Since I am discussing regional history museums, I have sought things I considered documents. Objects had to have direct, obvious, and irrefutable meaning about a place. The examples include museum purchases, gifts, and in one instance, what has to be the most unusual circumstances surrounding the totally unexpected arrival of a long-delayed bequest.

History museums exist to present information regarding the past that is considered by some to be important now and, optimistically, well into the future. These institutions use objects to confirm the veracity of whatever subject a particular museum exists for. This charge means things help certify the reality of person(s), place(s), idea(s), event(s), and so on. In application, the objects are quite literally viewed as three-dimensional documents of history. Their evidentiary role causes them to stand as proof, not simply props.

As with all museums, those devoted to history are appreciated by individuals passionate about the topic of the entity. When we count historic sites, multibuilding nonprofit assemblages and parks, and single structures designated for the sole purpose of preserving legacies of relevance, history museums number in the tens of thousands. There are far more history museums than there are museums of art or science. They range from small one-room historical societies open to the public on a limited schedule and run by volunteers to large complex entities with extensive and paid staff open to visitors on an almost daily basis. As public service institutions, these unusual inventions attempt to project high ideals, valued concepts, and major accomplishments to memorialize.

History museum content promotes a blend of facts, theories, and emotions about people, ideas, places, and events. The blend can be static or subject to flux, predictable or otherwise. What might be thought important now might be considered irrelevant someday. The reasoning behind what is collected, kept, studied, or in many cases ignored often depends on societal attitudes regarding a museum's mission and how that is best reflected in its collections.

There are history museums for an incredible variety of topics. Regardless of topic, however, they share a common aspiration. They have to determine what stuff has meaningful narrative value directly pertinent to their mission. How do history museum acquisition practices unfold? The following five examples illustrate my approach to collecting three-dimensional "data." Getting the objects was done by purchase, gift, or a combination thereof. These acquisitions represent typical ways of collecting. One, a racing car, was quickly suggested and obtained. Another, regarding prints, took a few years to unfold. A third, the purchase of a chair, happened internally without any involvement by non-museum-related supporters. The fourth, an outdoor sculpture garden, was an unanticipated opportunity not to be missed. The fifth, seven paintings by the self-taught artist Grandma Moses, was a gift with a unique gestation period, to say the least.

It is important to note that, with the exception of fine art, just about everything in history museums ceases its original function when it is accessioned (numbered and catalogued) into the collection. Usually a chair is no longer sat in. A piece of clothing is no longer worn. Airplanes are not flown. A tool ceases to be used. A bed is never slept in. Radios are silent. And so on. When an object becomes accessioned by a history museum, it morphs from its original function to fulfilling the aforementioned evidentiary role.

Each acquisition was possible because I was working in long-established, well-respected organizations. Few precarious museums or places pretending to be museums can collect responsibly or cultivate meaningful and enthusiastic interpersonal relationships that accrue to long-term benefit. Presumably what I collected will be around in perpetuity, to use a popular museum term.

Vroom, Vroom

The Western Reserve Historical Society in Cleveland, Ohio, is dedicated to preserving the history of the northeast quadrant of Ohio, referred in the eighteenth century as the western land reserve of Connecticut. The society has multiple components including two museums, a research library, and a historic house at its complex in Cleveland's University Circle. It also boasts an entire small historic village in Akron, Ohio. From 1991 to 1995 I had the pleasure of being the director of museums at the society.

One of the society's museums is the Crawford Auto Aviation Museum. It documents the fact that Cleveland was America's first car manufacturing center before it was eclipsed in the early twentieth century by Detroit. Most cars in the collection date from the first half of the twentieth century. Many were made in Cleveland. The region remained involved in the auto industry. There is also a long legacy of racing in particular.

At the time I was director, the car collection had two volunteer groups supporting its programming. Both had antique cars themselves and were well known within this collecting field. In looking at the museum's car holdings it was clear few new examples of regional automotive history were represented. I thought that was unfortunate and wanted to correct it somehow. Of course, it would be easy to just add cars owned or driven by local folks, but I expressed a desire to get something of notoriety for our visitors. I wanted a car that immediately stood out in our display and had documentary importance beyond mundane local ownership. I would occasionally hear about a race car driver named Bobby Rayhal. He was and remains quite famous in the sport.

Given the renown of Bobby Rayhal, I thought one of his racing cars might be an ideal acquisition for the museum. I had no idea if such a gift or purchase were possible. I floated the thought with the "car guys," as I informally referred to the two support groups (who were all men at that time). A few claimed to know the racer, or members of his pit crew, or family. I was never too sure if these claims had merit until one day one of the "car guys" said he had talked with Rayhal and he would love to give the museum a car. I was elated but knew to be careful regarding explanations about how a museum's professional protocols for a gift would be implemented. Prior to my arrival the car collection was handled in a very haphazard manner, as there was no professional curator. The "car guys" ran the operation as they thought best. Though well-meaning, their involvement hardly conformed to generally accepted museum practices.

I decided to let the Rayhal gift prospect unfold at its own pace (so to speak). I hoped the contact who told me of his conversation with the race car driver had relayed my message of glee and appreciation. He had. I was soon told the car would be forthcoming as an unrestricted gift once the owner prepared it for

Figure 10.1 82C Indy Cosworth Car. In 1982 Cleveland hosted a racing event that included such prominent names as Mario Andretti, Tom Sneva, Jonny Rutherford, Rick Mears, Al Unser Sr., A.J. Foyt, and Gordon Johncock. The race was the Budweiser-Cleveland 500 held at Burke Lakefront Airport on the Fourth of July weekend. Winner of the first Cleveland 500 Grand Prix Race. Second in the PPG Indy Car World Series. Bobby Rayhal — "Rookie of the Year." Gift of Mary and Richard Leppla. 93.45.1, Western Reserve Historical Society. (Photo Steven Miller.)

delivery. I had no idea what this meant or when it would occur but wisely keep quiet so as not to be disappointed should nothing happen.

One day I was in my office and received a call from the museum's admission desk. A car was being delivered. I immediately ran down to the automobile museum loading dock. The Rayhal car had already been wheeled onto the museum exhibition floor. It was in pristine condition, as the owner had decided to repaint and re-decal it to show both it and him at best advantage once in the museum. I was elated and thanked him. The necessary gift documentation was prepared. Our registrar made sure the requisite copies were signed and retained. When Rayhal and his crew departed, I quickly had a temporary label made and then met with our public relations office to prepare a press release.

Purposely and regularly collecting new things for a history museum is a fairly recent acquisition practice. I had initiated a program when I was a curator at the Museum of the City of New York. In pursuing this sort of acquisition the questions to ask are: What does an item document about the present and does that matter? Will the object be of interest to future generations, and what will it tell those generations about the past? These queries are not always as easily answered as might seem to be the case. With the Rayhal racer, though, I was confident it would be an excellent history messenger. I remain so and am only sorry I won't be around in a hundred years to have my hunch proved correct.

This was probably one of the easiest acquisitions I ever made. There were five essential reasons for success:

- I had indicated the collection had an important gap, and no one disagreed.
- As fortune dictated, one way to help fill the gap was presented with a new well-documented acquisition that fit the mission of the museum.
- The museum could accept the item – delivered – with no difficulties such as cost, onerous care burden, displacement of other collections, or acquisition restrictions.
- There was no deadline or schedule on the arrival of the object.
- Vehicles take up more space than most history museum collections. Fortunately there was room for the racer.
- In addition to having made the acquisition call, my final assignment was to show enthusiasm and say thank you when the object arrived.

Curatorial Gap-O-Sis

The late Joseph Veach Noble, when he was director of the Museum of the City of New York, once informed me of a terrible disease curators suffered from. Since I was an aspiring curator there, I paid immediate attention. He said the sickness was "Gap-o-sis." It was diagnosed as the severe need to fill gaps in whatever collections the curator was responsible for. I immediately admitted I suffered from this dreaded illness. In fact, our conversation at the time was about what I considered to be an astonishing gap in the museum's art collection. We had no paintings of the city by the famous American Ash Can School of artists or their corollary, The Eight. These were neither a place nor a club, but an informal group of like-minded artists. They did some of their most important work in the early years of the twentieth century in New York City. Spurning bucolic landscapes, decorative still life tableaus, formal society portraits, or academic imagery about classical myths and major historic events, they turned to the underbelly of the urban lives of ordinary people, especially where they worked or lived. The list of artists included John Sloan, Robert Henri, George Luks, Ernest Lawson, William J. Glackens, Arthur B. Davies, Everett Shinn, and Maurice Predergast. The Museum of the City of New York had no urban scenes by any of these men. It was, to my way of thinking, an outrageous gap.

Initially I had two questions about the absence of such important art: How did this happen and how could it be corrected? The answer to the first question was told to me by the then two living previous curators responsible for the museum's picture collections, Grace Mayer and Albert "Barry" Baragwanath. Grace was in charge of paintings, prints, and photographs virtually from the start of the museum. Barry was her successor. They both told me the same thing. What I inquired about was generally categorized as art and therefore it belonged in

Figure 10.2 John Sloan, *The Lafayette*, 1928. Etching with handwritten note to his New York City art dealer. John Kraushaar Collection, Museum of the City of New York, 84.120.1 Gift of Antoinette Kraushaar © 2021 Delaware Museum of Art Museum/Artists Rights Society (ARS) New York

art museums. The Museum of the City of New York was about history, and they wanted to collect images that precisely, not atmospherically, documented the past of the city. I liked these people very much. They were well educated, intelligent, personable, and knowledgeable mentors. However, I was (and remain) appalled by this curatorial blinder.

Having learned why the museum lacked paintings of importance by the Ash Can School or The Eight, I set about trying to correct the omission. That was easier said than done. Few of their pictures came on the commercial art market. Because I had no accession budget, this absence was of little consequence. Since most museum collections are donations, I sought individuals who collected these works. No one came to my attention (nor has yet!).

In thinking about how to avoid future historical gaps in the museum's collections, a practice I began for the department was to focus on getting new documentary pictures of New York. As a (nonexhibiting and nonselling) sculptor at the time, I enjoyed the contemporary art scene in the city and followed it closely. On occasion I would see new paintings, prints, and photographs that recorded aspects of the urban scene. I met some of the artists, and it was easy to persuade a few to donate work. Usually an exhibit initiated this generosity. I did a few and was especially pleased to promote artists previously also absent in the museum, notably people of color, those identifying as minorities, and women. History museums were not pursuing contemporary acquisitions at the time, so I was somewhat in the vanguard. In fact, I wrote a few essays for trade publications about the practice. Today it is not unusual, but back then mostly old things were taken in by history museums. As I proceeded with my regular agenda to acquire current documentary art, organize exhibits, initiate new conservation measures, and assist researchers, I still hoped to correct the historic picture collection imbalance.

One day I received a call from the museum's development office. A man was offering to make an unsolicited monetary donation. He was unknown to the museum. I asked if he had any particular interest in New York City history. He said he collected prints, so the department transferred him to me. At that time I had hoped to get new storage cabinets for the unframed paper-based picture collection. The price to purchase what I wanted was $25,000. The cabinets would replace about 100 running feet of 50-year-old wood cabinets. As my conversation with the gentleman unfolded and I explained my immediate needs, he offered to cover the cost. Hurrah! Needless to say I was delighted, and we proceeded to purchase the custom-made cabinets. They are still in use.

Following this fortuitous introduction, the donor would contact me every fall, and we would shop for prints to add to the collection. During that time I got to know Annette Kraushaar and her gallery of the same last name. She was good friends of the collector, and we mostly shopped there. During the course of our annual meetings I learned her father had been one of John Sloan's dealers. Ah-ha! Perhaps I had hit pay dirt in my quest for Ash Can School art. I explained our collection gap. She had no paintings and for whatever reason never seemed to carry them in the few years we worked together. But she did have prints. We bought some, and she gave us some. The ones she gave us were inscribed by the artist in pencil to her father. This made them a double treat. Not only were they important images of New York but they had a wonderful city provenance. The prints enjoy a prominent place at the museum and will continue to be important "art" about the city and its exciting past even if the subjects were considered somewhat pedestrian at the time. Sadly, the museum still does not have any major paintings by the artists I hoped to acquire.

The reasons we were able to attract the Kraushaar accessions were simple:

- All curators are wise to have a list of what they want for "their" collections. One never knows what happy circumstances may unfold going forward.
- Through a generous donor we had built a relationship with a key art dealer in our community. Of course, that donor bought art from the dealer, so it was in her best interest to continue to curry favor with him, but over time that was almost an immaterial consideration.

- The museum was well respected. There was little fear on the part of the donor that her contributions would be lost, sold, or otherwise misused.
- There was no question that the donation would be valued and appreciated by the museum and play an important role in correcting a past deficiency.

New York Now

Until recently most history museums rarely collected new objects, at least not with any disciplined regularity. There is too much of the past to preserve. When I was a curator at the Museum of the City of New York, I initiated a change in this habit as I sought to acquire contemporary images of the city. My challenge

Figure 10.3 Yonah Shimmel Knish Bakery, Hedy Pagremanski, 1976. Oil on canvas, Museum of the City of New York. Gift of the artist 1979.50

was twofold: What should we bring in that would be relevant to future generations and what can we logistically accommodate? My department handled paintings, prints, and photographs of New York City. I wanted to support living artists, especially those unrepresented or underrepresented by self-identifying gender, race, or ethnicity. I wanted to add examples of their documentary images to the collection for future appreciation. As previously noted, at the time, in addition to being a curator I was a sculptor who enjoyed the current urban art world. I would on occasion see paintings and prints depicting the city, and there were always photographs. For the museum the question was how to avoid an onslaught of this last category of art in particular. If I made an announcement that we were seeking pictures for the collection, we would be inundated with photos of all sorts.

History museum curators are anthropologists. Their studies are manifested through the collections for which they are responsible and/or acquire. I applied this approach to my new acquisition program. If New York City is known for anything, it is known for change. The "city that never sleeps" is always in some sort of flux. One of the best ways to prove this is by examining the history of its neighborhoods. They can change character in a generation.

In seeking art that documented places beginning to experience what would eventually be radical changes in character, I discovered an artist who was similarly devoted to capturing well-known sites rife for disappearance. She is Hedy Pagremanski.

She was born in Vienna, Austria, before the Nazis rose to power. As a Jewish "hidden" child, she was able to escape in 1938 along with her parents and brother. They arrived first in Panama. Hedy was able to later study art in Chicago before moving to New York City, where she continued her studies. In time she took up painting city scenes of places that were about to change or might. Most of her art depicts southern Manhattan. She especially enjoyed depicting buildings and businesses remaining from neighborhoods once predominately Jewish. One of the few surviving businesses from Manhattan's old Jewish Lower East Side is Yonah Schimmel's Knish Bakery. It is a New York City culinary landmark.

The people shown in Hedy's paintings are a signature element. Few are unknown. Because she paints on the street, in an urban plein air tradition, her work is admired and commented upon by passersby. If they have an affiliation with the place being captured on canvas, the artist often puts them in the picture after recording their identities and connections. Indeed, I appear in one of her paintings. This unusual documentary practice only adds to the historical value of her paintings.

I could acquire this painting because:

- It conformed ideally with my new collecting agenda and focus.
- It was available.
- It was offered as an unrestricted gift from the artist.
- I did not have to get anyone's permission or approval within the museum to acquire it.

Posthumous Portraits

During my tenure as executive director of Boscobel Restoration, Inc., in Garrison, New York, our board of trustee chair would periodically assign me a project. Most were benign and of little importance. A couple had a lasting impact. While I generally dislike trustee intrusions into museum operations, I had no reason to disagree with any of his particular directives, and we got along very well. Had I expressed opposition, problems would have ensued. The chair and the board had a reputation for doing things without professional staff input. This practice led to some costly decisions, but since the endowment was so ample, no one balked at the financial hit. It wasn't their money. They never had to provide any financial support. Should an employee vigorously question trustee instructions, he or she would quickly be looking for work. Indeed, a previous director had been fired for objecting to a new building plan the chair had put forth only a few years ago.

Figure 10.4 Installing the Hudson River School Artists Garden. Boscobel Restoration, Garrison, New York, 2017. (Sculpture by Gregg Wyatt, photo by Steven Miller.)

(Fortunately it was so costly it went unrealized, though $300,000 was spent on architectural plans.)

Boscobel is a reproduction of a c. 1810 Federal period historic house. It overlooks the Hudson River in Garrison, New York. The view is stunning. One day as the board chair and I walked the property, he handed me an 8 × 10 color photograph. It showed some cast bronze portrait busts on pedestals. They were artists identified with the Hudson River School, which is not a place but a nineteenth-century American art movement. Our chairman said we should get them for Boscobel and place them at a spot he pointed to in front of our visitor center. I had no idea what he was talking about but immediately agreed to pursue the matter, as I liked the concept. He did not give me the name of the artist, contact information, or anything about the subject of the photograph other than that it was taken at the Canadian Embassy in Washington, D.C., where he had been that week.

Immediately after our meeting I called the Canadian Embassy for information. The busts were done by an American artist named Greg Wyatt whose studio was at the Newington Cropsey Foundation in Hastings-on-Hudson. The location is, conveniently, about 40 miles downriver from Boscobel. I called Greg and arranged a studio visit for our board chair and me. I wanted to see if the art was any good, if his work was appropriate for Boscobel, if the chair's exhibition scheme made sense. If all was copasetic, how could the project be executed competently and in a timely and secure manner? Cost was also a consideration. I had no sense of its price.

Our meeting with the artist was very positive. Greg is a respected and accomplished representational sculptor who works in a traditional academic style. He has a distinguished resume of outdoor projects in particular. It is one thing to make sculpture for a specific exterior site and quite another for it to be done safely and effectively. Greg's outdoor projects are ideally arranged and installed. Matters of scale, appearance, and multiple visual perspectives are handled beautifully. In addition to being assured the project would be completed to Boscobel's satisfaction, we were delighted to be told all expenses would be paid for by the Newington Cropsey Foundation.

The proposed placement of the sculpture was ideal. I was similarly enthusiastic about the concept of celebrating America's first national art movement, the hub of which was the Hudson Highlands around Garrison. As a museum acquisition, the sculpture project was serendipitous. Prior to our board chair's suggestion, I had no thoughts of including the Hudson River School art or artists in our permanent programming. We had done exhibitions of some less-than-famous acolytes of the movement but were otherwise content to let major American art museums feature their work.

The plan outlined by Greg was superb and ideally suited to expanding Boscobel's museum scope. The fact that the artist sculpted posthumous portraits is immaterial. He reliably and with great attention examined historical photographs and whatever physical descriptions were available. The subjects represent the most famous of the artists of this school. As such they meld both the physical setting the artist selected and the chronological story his art tells.

Once it was decided the project made sense for Boscobel, I had to figure out how to implement it. Talk is cheap in the museum field. Wise, timely, affordable, competent, and nondestructive action is another matter. The reasons we could get this unusual acquisition were several:

- It was mission appropriate.
- As the board chair's idea, no other trustees disagreed. The only people who could effectively contradict him were those he thought socially and financially his betters. No one really cared about this project, and any that might oppose it had no backbone. It is important to note that he had been chair for decades, which is highly unusual in the museum field and considered completely out of line for good governance.
- I wrote the agreement with the Newington Foundation to let the sculptor proceed unimpeded and solely under his direction. It included a $10,000/year payment to Boscobel for ten years for maintenance.
- The project did not financially, physically, or programmatically encumber Boscobel.
- The sculptor was extremely accomplished as both an artist and a designer and installer of his works.
- The sculptor's plans for the site included the precise location of each sculpture and terrain and planting requirements and configurations (severely altered by a subsequent administration).
- I was able to cordon off the site and let the artist work at his own pace with his own employees. There was no requirement for Boscobel staff participation, and I created signage to explain the project to the public.
- Maintenance of the sculpture was minimal and thus of no added institutional burden.

Have a Seat

People tend to think historic house museums are somewhat static when it comes to their collections. While this may be the case for "time capsule" homes preserved with most or all of their original contents intact, it is not necessarily true of those furnished conjecturally or treated as nonhistorical interiors subject to changes in furnishings, décor, or other content whenever an organization wishes. The home of Frederick Edwin Church in Catskill, New York. is a perfect example of a property that has not changed its fundamental interiors since the artist and his family lived there. Boscobel Restoration, Inc., in Garrison, New York, on the other hand, is a perfect example of a completely fictional historic site. The building is essentially a reproduction of a c. 1810 Federal-style structure that was originally located much farther down river. Pieces of it were retrieved in a last-ditch effort to preserve some of it. The salvaged parts were trucked 60 miles upriver to be incorporated into a new structure at a gorgeous location overlooking the Hudson River and surrounding landscape. It was rebuilt according to architectural plans of the original house drawn in the 1930s. The rooms are a curatorial idea of early

Figure 10.5 Side Chair, c. 1815, New York City; possibly by Duncan Phyfe. Mahogany with modern upholstery. Collection of Boscobel House and Gardens. Purchased by exchange, 2013.01 courtesy of Boscobel House & Gardens

nineteenth-century New York City high-style interiors. Though make-believe, the house boasts one of the best small collections of American Federal-style furniture.

When I became executive director of Boscobel in 2013, everyone assumed the interior was a static display. As much as I love acquisitions, nothing needed to be added. Nevertheless, unexpected but happily, opportunities arose. The first year I was there we replaced the wallpaper in the grand entry hall. The period-appropriate reproduction paper put up c. 1976 had been installed upside down! The replacement period-appropriate reproduction paper was made the way wallpaper would have been made in the early nineteenth century. The multicolor design was block printed on square sheets rather than being silkscreened on rolls, as was previously the case. A new floor covering was also made and installed, again, according to a period-appropriate design.

After the hall renovation no further changes occurred in the house until three years later when a chair came up for auction. A trustee brought it to my attention. It was perfect for the time period depicted in the house and was a design not represented. He was a former American furniture curator at the Metropolitan Museum of Art. His specialty was the era depicted at Boscobel and the cabinet maker to whom the chair is attributed.

I visited the New York City auction house handling the sale and examined the chair. There were actually a pair, and they matched duplicate chairs in another museum collection. Both were undamaged and original except for the upholstery, which was historically correct. I immediately got the museum's collection committee to approve having me bid on one of the chairs. We had no interest in getting both. Meetings of the group were unnecessary, as emails and phone calls sufficed. I bid by phone from my office with our curator present. We were successful. There was some competition, and thus the price was high and far above what would be expected now with the dip in market value of these antiques.

There were seven key reasons we were able to add the chair to our collections and thus expand the scope of our stylistic holdings for this period of American interior design:

- It was appropriate to our mission.
- It represented an upgrade in our holdings.
- We had an acquisition budget provided with funds from deaccessions.
- No one set an auction bid limit for me.
- We had the best expertise in the field recommending the purchase. This is probably one reason there were no complaints about how much we paid for the chair.
- We could move the formal acquisition process along quickly.
- We had a good reputation in the art and antiques business that allowed us to bid without difficulty.

Welcome Home Grandma . . . Finally

One afternoon in February 1998 a four-foot-square wooden crate was delivered to the Bennington Museum. It was addressed to me as executive director. I was not expecting any deliveries. It was brought to my attention by our curator when she almost tripped over the box in the mailing area of our offices. When we opened it we found seven paintings by the famous self-taught artist commonly known as Grandma Moses. A cryptic note accompanied them, but it offered no indication of the source of the paintings or why they had been sent to the museum. The return address was a commercial shipping center in Quakertown, Pennsylvania.

The Bennington Museum is the center for art by Grandma Moses, whose name was Anna Mary Robertson Moses (1860–1961). She was a farmwife who lived

Figure 10.6 Anna Mary Robertson Moses (Grandma Moses), *Vermont*, 1958. Oil on Masonite. Bennington Museum, 1998. Bequest of Margaret M. Carr © Grandma Moses Properties, New York.

for a few years in Bennington, as well as across the state line in New York and also in Virginia. An excellent knitter, she was encouraged to switch to painting when arthritis made that craft difficult. At 70 she began doing oil paint landscapes on Masonite, recording local scenes and rural activities she recalled from her youth. Otto Kallir, a New York City art dealer, discovered her art when he saw it in a Hoosick Falls, New York, hardware store window. He immediately recognized a marketable talent. She soared to fame after he started promoting her at his Gallerie St. Etienne in Manhattan.

As we puzzled in surprise about the box and its contents, our registrar, who had been with the museum for about 20 years, recalled notifications we had received years before regarding a bequest of Moses pictures. She checked her files. Sure enough, a woman in Pennsylvania, near Quakertown, had willed the museum seven Grandma Moses paintings. Before the paintings could be packed and delivered to Bennington, her house had been broken into and the pictures stolen.

Rather than assume the newly delivered box contained the long-delayed bequest, several measures were in order. First we called the Art Loss Register to report what was presumably the discovery of stolen art. The organization had no information on the theft in question or the particular pictures. At the same time we called Gallerie St. Etienne to alert it and help secure our ownership. I then contacted Robert Whitman at the Federal Bureau of Investigation's art theft office.

The gallery appreciated my call. They confirmed it had no ownership rights to the pictures, only reproduction rights, as it has with all Moses paintings. Whitman came to the museum and inspected the crate, note, and pictures. He told an interesting story about the presumed source.

Apparently at the time of the theft from the deceased's home in Pennsylvania, two brothers were breaking into houses in the area and hiding stolen goods in their home basement. It had been renovated to essentially act as a private vault. Not long before the museum received its paintings, the brothers had a falling out. When one threatened to report their activities to the police, the other one scrambled to get rid of incriminating evidence.

When we were certain the Bennington Museum was the rightful owner of the art, we enjoyed releasing the news to the media. It made for a fascinating story, though one without mention of the robbers, as their legal entanglements were still being sorted out by investigators and attorneys.

This was certainly the most unusual acquisition I have ever encountered on the job. When it finally unfolded as originally intended, there were a few important reasons for a smooth and successful transition:

- The museum had a key employee who had been there for years in the office holding relevant records. And the records were still there.
- Staff knew who to contact immediately to assess the legitimacy of the delivery and thus protect the museum against any legal or related imbroglios.
- The original owner knew the museum was the ideal repository for her largess.
- There is no honor among thieves.

11 Barnum Brown's Bones

Douglas J. Preston

Dinosaurs in the Attic: An Excursion into the American Museum of Natural History
St. Martin's Press, NY, 1986 pp. 65–72

The American Museum of Natural History is in New York City. It was founded in 1869 by a group of wealthy philanthropists who had an interest in studying and preserving a global collection of flora and fauna representing as much of the world as possible at the time. Today it is one of the preeminent museums of natural history with collections numbering in the millions. In addition to galleries that are especially popular with families and children, it is a major research center for subjects related to its vast collections.

The dinosaur exhibits are probably the best known aspect of the museum. They contain a vast array of the remains of both peculiar and ordinary creatures that once existed. Standout holdings feature dinosaurs. The museum's website estimates it has about 400,000 mammal fossils (www.amnh.org/research/paleontology).

At the time of its formation the museum had no fossils. This absence was to dramatically change largely because of one person whose passion, expertise, tireless energy, cunning, scholarly diligence, intuition in the field, and hard work, not to mention luck, caused the museum to acquire the core collection of what it has today. Naturally this person enjoyed sufficient funding and support from museum leaders to do his job as he saw fit. The man was Barnum Brown. He was with the museum nearly 50 years. This chapter is an excerpt from Douglas J. Preston's book about the museum published in 1986. In it he tells the fascinating story of Brown.

There are very few books about science museums written for the general museum field. There are even fewer narrative accounts about how those museums collect. The story of Brown's work is therefore of special value, and I am grateful to the author for writing his book and permitting this chapter.

When Barnum Brown arrived at the American Museum in 1897 at the age of twenty-three, the Museum possessed not a single dinosaur. When he died in 1963, just one week shy of his ninetieth birthday, it was chock-full of them, the largest and best collection in the world. Many of the Museum's finest specimens – including the superb *Tyrannosaurus rex* – were discovered by Brown during his

Figure 11.1 Tyrannosaurus rex skeleton, American Museum of Natural History, New York City. Collected by B. Brown and P.C. Kaisen, 1908, Big Dry Creek, Montana, USA. (Photo by Steven Miller, 2021.)

sixty-six-year career. He worked in every major geographical area of the world except Japan, Australia, Madagascar and the South Sea Islands. To get to and from those places with his picks and whisk booms, he once said he had used every available form of transportation except the submarine. Of the two dinosaur halls in the Museum, one, the Hall of Late Dinosaurs, is a virtual monument to Barnum Brown, as he collected most of its skeletons.

Brown found most of his dinosaurs in Western North America, and he became something of a celebrity. Wherever he went, he was feted by the local populace, who came in droves to meet his train, and who would vie for the honor of having him in their carriage. Called "Mr. Bones" by both press and public, Brown's ability to locate dinosaurs became legendary. A scientist wrote that he could "smell fossils, even though they had been buried 100 million years."

A paleontologist locates fossils in much the same way a sophisticated prospector locates minerals. The fossil hunter begins with an extensive knowledge of geology and a deep study of the geological landscape of the area to be searched. Usually the hunter will try to follow sedimentary beds known to contain fossils across intervening strata to an unexplored outcrop. Like the prospector, the fossil hunter tends to rely on intuition and even hunches to locate fossils, as well as such hearsay evidence as idle bar conversation, chats with ranchers, oilmen, and prospectors, and so forth.

But like the prospector, the fossil hunter combines this with his knowledge of geology to make a strike. For example, an up-fold of strata (called an anticline) is often an excellent formation in which to find fossils. Usually the top of the anticline is eroded away. If fossils have been found on one side of the anticline, where a particular layer of rock has been exposed, one can usually find similar fossils on the other side. However, the other side may be many miles away, with complex terrain in between. The great fossil hunter can map out the intervening terrain and pinpoint where that particular fossiliferous layer will reappear on the far side.

Brown was a complex man. A photograph in the Museum's archives, taken at a remote site in the desolate badlands of Wyoming, shows him in a magnificent and costly fur coat, gravely examining a fossil through his gold-rimmed pince-nez. He usually dressed impeccably for the field, and one of his crew members who had worked with him as a youth said, "Woe to the boy who spilled plaster of Paris on his shiny boots." One colleague reported that he was an accomplished ballroom dancer, in great demand among the ladies. Another said that Brown's "grave, sometimes melancholy countenance" suggested the mien of a Presbyterian minister. Like many great explorers, he was an indifferent scientist. He cared little about publishing his finds, and his colleagues often gently upbraided him for it.

Barnum Brown was born in Carbondale, Kansas, in 1873. His parents had moved to Kansas by wagon train before the Civil War and had built a pioneer cabin, which later grew into a rather prosperous farm with side businesses. His parents named him, somewhat prophetically, after the great showman P.T. Barnum, because as Brown explained later, it added alliterative interest to his dull surname. As a boy he would follow farmers' plows through the fields of Carbondale, picking up the hundreds of fossils shells turned up by the blades. His collection eventually filled the laundry building on the family farm. At the University of Kansas he met Professor Samuel Williston, Marsh's former head dinosaur hunter, who introduced him into that arcane profession. In 1896 he came to the Museum to work part-time on a fossil prospecting party, and the following year the Museum brought him on staff.

Henry Fairfield Osborn had plans to make the American Museum the foremost repository for vertebrate fossils and, indeed, the center of fossil vertebrate research in the world. In many ways Osborn was to vertebrate paleontology what Boas was to anthropology; just as Boas is called the father of American anthropology, Osborn was named the father of vertebrate paleontology. He was mainly interested in fossil mammals; but he knew that it was the mounted skeletons of dinosaurs, more than mammals, that would attract attention, publicity, and money to the Museum. In the summer of 1897, Osborn sent Brown and a collecting party to Como Bluff, Wyoming, to explore the Upper Jurassic beds where Othniel C. Marsh had earlier made spectacular discoveries.

Perseverance, however, paid off in the end. Later that summer Osborn himself arrived to inspect the site, and he and Brown explored a nearby bluff. Brown noticed some bones weathering out of an outcrop, and the two men examined them with mounting excitement. The bones were undoubtedly saurian – the Museum's first dinosaur. Brown and another member of the expedition traced these fossil-bearing beds to an unexplored outcrop known as the Medicine Bow Anticline – and here they struck pay dirt. A photograph in the Museum's archives showing the unexcavated spot gives an idea of just how rich this area was. It reveals a hillside strewn with hundreds of dinosaur bones – more common than the surrounding rocks. The bones lay about in such profusion that, years before, a sheepherder had built an entire cabin out of them. Naturally, the locality became known as Bone Cabin Quarry.

This site yielded some of the most impressive dinosaurs yet discovered. In 1898 the Museum party cut into the hillside and surrounding strata, and over the next six years they uncovered dinosaur after dinosaur. In the fall of 1898 alone they shipped thirty tons of bones in boxcars to New York; in 1899, another twenty tons; in 1900, ten tons; and in the last year of excavation, when everyone had begun to complain that the quarry was petering out, they brought back five more tons.

During the excavations, some of the paleontologists took side trips to outcrops of the same formations, hoping for another mother lode of fossils. In 1898, some five miles south of the Bone Cabin Quarry, at place known as Nine Mile Crossing of Little Medicine Creek, Walter Granger, one of Osborn's paleontologists, discovered a promising site where some bones had weathered out of the rock. The succeeding summer they established a separate camp and started removing the fossil – a magnificent *Brontosaurus*.

It was an exceedingly difficult excavation because of the size and weight of the specimen (the right thigh bone alone weighed 570 pounds). Enormous blocks of matrix (the stone in which a fossil is embedded) were quarried out of the bank and shipped to the Museum, where it took another two years to chip way the matrix, piece together the brittle, shattered bone, cement it, and restore areas of missing bone. Another three years passed while the skeleton was being mounted, and when at last it went on display in the Museum, it was the largest fossil skeleton ever mounted anywhere.

As with most mounted dinosaurs, missing bones were either replaced with fossils from other finds or modeled in plaster. Even though the *Brontosaurus* was unusually complete, it required bones from Como Bluff and vertebrae and toe bones from Bone Cabin Quarry to fill the gaps; various other bones were modeled in plaster after specimens in the Yale Museum.

Unfortunately, an exhaustive search failed to turn up a skull for the *Brontosaurus*. This was not the first time such a thing had happened. Marsh, the original discoverer of the *Brontosaurus* (now correctly termed *Apatosaurus*), had first described the animal from a headless skeleton found in 1879. But in his haste to beat Cope, he had crowned the creature with a restoration made from two fragmentary skulls found miles from the site. Osborn accepted Marsh's restoration, and topped his *Brontosaurus* with a cast of the March skull. In 1915, however, Earl Douglas, a paleontologist from the Carnegie Museum of Natural History in Pittsburgh, discovered a *Brontosaurus* skeleton with a completely different skull right underneath it. Douglas suggested in a paper that Marsh might have given his *Brontosaurus* the wrong skull. Perhaps because this challenged the Museum's reconstruction, of which Osborn was so proud, Osborn, "in a bantering mood" (Douglas said), dared the Carnegie paleontologist to pick a scientific fight with the great and powerful Osborn, and he never did mount his skull – or *any* skull. The Carnegie *Brontosaurus* went headless until Douglas' death in 1932, when a copy of the Marsh head was finally mounted.

Not until 1975 did anyone step forward to challenge the Marsh skull. Finally, two paleontologists (one at Carnegie) published a paper maintaining that the Marsh skull was entirely incorrect and should be replaced by the Douglas skull. The evidence they presented was overwhelmingly persuasive. In 1979 the Carnegie museum decapitated their *Brontosaurus* and crowned it with the much more graceful Douglas skull. Other museums followed suit. The American Museum has intended to replace *its* wrong skull and obtained a copy from the Carnegie Museum. Unfortunately, an examination of the Museum's *Brontosaurus* mount revealed that any head-switching would be risky unless the entire skeleton was restored. So – for the time being, at least – the old skull is still in place, topping the great *Brontosaurus* in the Museum's Hall of Early Dinosaurs.

Getting back to Barnum Brown: Brown continued to scour the West, working quarries and prospecting. While Jurassic dinosaurs were being pulled out of Bone Cabin Quarry, Brown stuck fossil gold in another location – Hell Creek, Montana. These were Upper Cretaceous beds, dating from the apex of the Age of the Dinosaurs, and in 1902 Brown organized a Museum expedition to the Hell Creek formation. His nose proved unerring. Buried in the sandstone matrix he discovered the skeleton of a huge carnivorous dinosaur, previously unknown to science. The sandstone was exceptionally hard, and the fossil had to be dynamited out of its tomb. Tons of sandstone blocks containing rare fossils were hauled from the site by horse-drawn wagon 130 miles to the nearest railroad. When finally assembled, this grim meat-eater was christened *Tyrannosaurus rex*, "King of the Tyrant Lizards."

Five years later at Hell Creek, Brown found another *Tyrannosaurus* in superb condition. The Museum kept both tyrannosaurs, which were the only two reasonably complete skeletons of this dinosaur that had even been found, and were considered a national treasure. During World War II, when it was feared the Germans might bomb New York, the Museum donated the first *Tyrannosaurus* to the Carnegie Museum in Pittsburgh, where it remains to this day.

By the end of 1908, Brown had more or less cleaned out Hell Creek beds, and he started casting about for a third locale. Again, his luck held out. One day a talkative visitor from Canada showed up in his office. The man owned a large ranch along the Red Deer River in Alberta, and he mentioned that he had picked up bones along the banks of the Red Deer just like the bones on display in the Museum. Although Brown was somewhat skeptical, he nevertheless paid a visit to the ranch in 1909. One visit was all Brown needed. The rancher had collected a mass of bones, and most were saurian.

Brown immediately organized an expedition, which arrived at the valley of the Red Deer River in the early summer of 1910. Getting to the fossils – and getting them out – proved a difficult problem. The fossils were eroding out of the steep canyons along the river, and were thus inaccessible from the top. The only option available, Brown decided, was to float down the river on a barge big enough to carry his crew and all the fossils they would collect. They constructed a twelve-by-thirty-foot flatboat topped with a large canvas tent. The barge included such amenities as a cook stove (with chimney), and a canvas rowboat for shore landings. The thing was controlled with two large oarlike "sweeps," used for steering the boat through rapid water.

The party started downriver from Red Deer, scanning the canyon walls for signs of fossils. At first they found only scattered mammalian remains, but at the bend of the river near Content, Alberta, the walls began yielding dinosaurs in increasing numbers. As they lazily floated along, Brown would scan the canyon walls with binoculars, and the crew would then land at promising sites. The dinosaurs kept rolling in. "Box after box," Brown wrote, "was added to the collection until scarcely a cubit's space remained unoccupied on board our fossil ark."

After the Canadian expedition, the next two decades were quiet ones for Brown. He diversified his collecting activities and traveled the world, finding everything from mummified musk ox to fossil turtles. Then came the 1930s, and with them the discovery for which Brown is perhaps best remembered – the gigantic dinosaur graveyard at Howe Ranch. In 1931, Brown had led prospecting parties to the Lower Cretaceous beds of Montana, following the fossil-bearing rock southward to Greybill, Wyoming. Here he ran into a Mrs. Austin, herself a fossil enthusiast, who told him about some large bones she had seen on the Howe Ranch, at the base of the Bighorn Mountains. Two years later, Brown and several companions reconnoitered the ranch, and were guided to the big bones by a crusty eighty-two-year-old rancher named Barker. They were hard to miss; the bones were weathering out of a horizontal strata of rock adjacent to the ranch buildings. During the next week, Barker looked on while Brown painstakingly chipped away at the bones with his crooked awl to get a sense of what was there. A week of this was almost too much for Barker. Disgusted by the slowness of the work, he had to be physically restrained from hacking at the bones with a pickaxe. Brown realized that at least two large sauropod skeletons were embedded in the rock, but his limited team and financial resources made excavating impossible.

Large sums of money would be needed to recover the skeletons, and Brown turned to an old supporter, the Sinclair Oil Company, whose logo is, of course, a dinosaur. Readers may remember the dinosaur booklets and stickers that the Sinclair Oil Company gave out to motorists during the 1930s and 1940s. Brown wrote the booklets, while Sinclair bankrolled many of his expeditions.

In 1934, a much bigger expedition led by Brown returned to the Howe Ranch, and on June 1 they began uncovering the quarry to bedrock. Brown wrote:

> It soon became apparent that . . . there was a veritable herd of dinosaurs, their skeletal remains crossed, crisscrossed, and interlocked in a confused and almost inextricable manner. . . . Through the warping of the strata incident

to the nearby mountain uplift, the bones had been checked and fractured to a high degree, so all had to be thoroughly shellacked as soon as uncovered. Never have I seen such a thirsty lot of dinosaurs.

After the length and breadth of the bone deposit was determined, the area was gridded into three-foot squares. The bones were in such a tangle that all had to be drawn *in situ* first, and the relationships of the body sections mapped out before anything could be removed. To accomplish this, a man was hoisted in an old barrel about thirty feet above the quarry, from which photographs could be taken straight down on the tangle of bones.

Fortunately the bones were embedded in soft clay, and work progressed quickly. Finally, on November 17, the last crate of fossils was loaded into a boxcar bound for New York City. Packed into the car were 4,000 bones in 144 cases weighing 35 tons. At least twenty, and probably more, dinosaurs were represented by individual bones and entire skeletons. Most of the dinosaurs were the swamp-dwelling kind – the large bodied, long-necked sauropods.

The Howe Quarry presented a mystery. Never had such a concentration of dinosaur bones been discovered before. The bones were not water-worn or abraded, as would be expected if the Howe Quarry had been an eddy in an ancient stream bed. Nor had the bones been separated or scattered by scavengers. The bones were extensively interlocked, indicating that a single event may have killed them all at approximately the same time.

Even the distribution of bones was odd. Around the edges of the quarry were scattered single bones from smaller species, but in the center, a dozen limbs of large species were found standing upright on articulated feet. Surrounding the bones was a very fine silt of the kind deposited only in standing muddy water.

Brown studied the quarry and drew his own conclusions, which is more notable for the image it conjured up than for its accuracy. The following passage, published in *Natural History* in 1935, did much to shape our conception of the last days of dinosaurs.

> The climate was tropical, and we see flat land rich in vegetation, dotted by countless shallow lakes and marshes. Cycads, palms, and palmettos cover the lowlands, with pines on the uplands. Countless ferns, thick grass, and rushes form a rank vegetation over the marshy, hummocked shores. . . . [The dinosaurs] congregate by thousands, huddling close together as reptiles do, and filling every lagoon as far as the eyed can see.
>
> Now Mother Earth changes the stage setting. The impulse that finally was expressed by the nearby mountains elevated these lowlands. The large lakes were drained and the swamps vanished. The dinosaurs became more and more concentrated in the remaining pools as they were pushed together in huge herds. . .
>
> As the water recede, the smaller, weaker dinosaurs were trampled and their bones scattered on the borders of the pool; the larger ones huddled closer and closer together as they made their last futile stand against fate.

Brown's description is somewhat off the mark. The quarry probably represents the remains of a herd of dinosaurs that perished in a drying lake. However, it was a local phenomenon, not a worldwide extinction, since these were Jurassic dinosaurs, which lived relatively early in the Age of Dinosaurs. The event that caused the drying of the lake was probably nothing more than a severe drought, not the uplifting of the land, which usually takes millions of years.

Brown retired from the Museum in 1942, but continued to work until the week before his death in 1963. In his later years, as he conducted visitors through the fossil halls of the Museum, he would murmur, "Here's another one of my children." While he was planning a trip to the Isle of Write to dig dinosaurs out of its 800-foot cliffs (and while the Museum was planning his ninetieth birthday bash), Barnum Brown died.

His "children" can still be seen – the ponderous *Brontosaurus*, the *Tyrannosaurus*, and dozens of others, their huge, shellacked skeletons a memorial to the greatest dinosaur collector of them all.

Exhibition Label, American Museum of Natural History, 2021

> *"Personalities in Paleontology*
> *Barnum Brown (1873–1963*
>
> *The greatest dinosaur hunter of the twentieth century was Barnum Brown, who began his career at the American Museum in 1897 as an assistant to Henry Fairfield Osborn. Brown traveled all over the world collecting dinosaurs and fossil mammals. Some consider him to be the last of the great dinosaur hunters.*
>
> *Brown was always impeccably dressed, often wearing a tie and topcoat even in the field. He was a shrewd 'horse trader' when it came to wheeling and dealing for fossil specimens. Many of Brown's greatest discoveries are displayed in these halls, including the first specimens of Tyrannosaurus rex ever found. Barnum Brown died in new York in 1963, at the age of 89."*

12 Conclusion

Steven Miller

Ideas cause museums. But who concocts the ideas and why, when, where, and how? The answers have varied since museums were invented. Because there has never been a worldwide regulatory body dictating their format, these places are diverse in type, look, content, governance, purpose, and location. Regardless of their many differences, museums as we know them share one essential unique characteristic: they rely on the physical for validation. Having objects (often in abundance) to rationalize their existence has caused museums to assemble what everyone calls collections.

The best museum collections are, to borrow the historian's language, primary documents. In other words, art, artifacts, or scientific specimens are acquired because they have an original, direct connection to aspects of a particular subject. Objects of secondary or tertiary connectivity are either avoided, obtained by mistake, brought in for political reasons, or held without knowledge of their inapplicability. The acquisition examples discussed by the authors in this book fall into the primary category of collection assembly.

Museum collections happen by purchase, donation, exchange, excavation, and retrieval from nature. When obtained wisely, they have intrinsic importance that makes them of singular value on their own and relationally with other collections. Few objects in a museum are stand-alone possessions orphaned from what else a museum owns. Sadly, when acquired in a haphazard manner detached from an organization's core objective, collections are lies and burdens. I include what I consider an egregious example later in this chapter.

There has long been an assumption voiced by some that museums were cosseted enclaves exclusively appreciated and supported by specialists in whatever subject a museum was about. That accusation was accompanied by claims that museums were the private domain of sociopolitical-economic forces reflecting a mainstream power elite. In the United States, this elite was largely male, white, Protestant, and of Northern European ancestry, though it included a few women, Roman Catholics, and Jews who passed muster by attending prestigious prep schools and Ivy League colleges, marrying into the fold, or having wealth. It was never substantiated whether the general public was aware of all this or even cared, though accusers assumed so and still do. The so-called privileged-clubhouse atmosphere museums exuded was said to be reflected in their collections,

DOI: 10.4324/9781003216384-13

where objects presumably mirrored the interests of the power elite. Today that accusation is resulting in diverse collecting initiatives. Several are presented by these authors.

People who saw museums as antagonistic to democratic values concocted a meme to support their opinions. Whether those opinions were based on historic fact was immaterial, since museums have accepted the accusations and are now slowly addressing their actual (or perceived) exclusionary behaviors. Part of the corrective action involves collections. Critiques now abound over what was acquired, why, and how – and, going forward, what should be acquired, why, and how.

Without question, the most radical era of museum change erupted in the 1960s. Its effects are still unfolding. Initial impacts dramatically altered traditional ideas of museums, at least when it came to media postures officials tried to promote. During this tumultuous decade and the one following it, museums decided one way to shed allegations of fustiness was to borrow some of the management practices of performance halls, sports stadia, malls, amusement parks, and tourist attractions. The approach of operating as an attraction worked. Museums became quite popular and in ways never before imagined as entities focused on attendance. This remains an all-consuming task, and not just for museum workers. Outside interests vociferously pressure institutions about whom they seem to be addressing and, more importantly, whom they fail to care about. Collections are not immune from these conversations.

Museums take longer to effectively transform than one might expect or hope. In spite of dramatic changes usually manifested architecturally with new buildings, renovations, additions, and so on, substantive museum transition more likely happens at a glacial pace. Occasional spurts are suggested by newsworthy acquisitions.

For the most part, the outcome of altering museum operational thinking has been phenomenal insofar as their growth in numbers, popularity, size, and prominence globally. Reliable finite statistics are hard to come by given the hidden and untrustworthy nature of some countries' informational access, especially in lands under the thumb of dictators. Dipping into the world of academia provides an easy way to assess how much has changed in the museum field. When I landed my first job in 1971, the United States had three major graduate programs in what was becoming known as museum studies. To be sure, there were graduate programs in art history, science, and history that attracted students who might later work in museums, but these were cul-de-sac learning forums with little or no discussion of museums per se. Today there are scores of graduate programs to support museum careers. A parallel indication of museum proliferation is obvious by the thousands of books available regarding all sorts of aspects about what museums are and how they do or should do their jobs. Again, when I started my career, there were few. Oddly, with the exception of contemporary art, only a handful of books at best discuss collecting specifically.

Before the current turmoil in the museum field surfaced, their collections rarely caused much of a fuss when it came to ownership or content. Acquisition decisions were particularly of little interest, though cheers would be voiced when the arrival of some obviously stellar object was proudly announced. Today museum collecting activities are subject to a range of new opinions and pressures. The fact that this noise comes largely from outside their walls shows how museums are now lead players in all sorts of entertainment, political, economic, social, education, and cultural sectors. The centrality museums have come to assume has caused a meteoric rise in judgments about what they should collect. The acquisition stories provided herein offer insightful examples of traditional as well as new issues in collecting.

Over the years, I have come to the conclusion that deciding what a museum should collect in an ongoing, logical, and precise manner can be difficult, sometimes exceedingly so. The challenges are scholastic as well as practical. There is a lot of stuff in the universe. Most will not be acquired by museums. This is a good thing for so many reasons. How much of the tangible requires physical preservation? Indeed, I wonder how much of what I acquired for museums will be retained. To my knowledge, nothing has been jettisoned so far. Yet in time, assuming the museums holding these things still exist as they do now, generations following me may wonder what on earth Steven Miller was thinking when he took in such-and-such an item. Could my personal profile as a white, Anglo-Saxon, Protestant, and heterosexual male cause successors to assume my collecting practices showed a gross demographic exclusionary bias?

As illustrated by this volume's authors, museum collecting, obviously, is done by people. Because individual initiatives, tastes, job circumstances, and demands differ, museum collecting decisions differ. The universe of these participants is wonderfully diverse. Individuals making acquisition decisions can be spot-on in their work or woefully out to lunch. I believe without question the former is the case herein.

For the most part, I have always enjoyed my museum colleagues. The authors who have so generously contributed to this volume provide excellent examples of why. Some were known to me when I started organizing the book; others I first met when they enthusiastically responded to my call for essays. Our conversations and informational exchanges and their chapters simply confirm why I like being in the museum world. The acquisitions they made present, to my way of thinking, model approaches to this fundamental museum duty. There is no question these people understand how museums best meet their missions.

Alas, some in the museum field fail to reflect the thinking embraced by the authors assembled here. These individuals are often in positions of power, where harm can be done, and too often their influence on museum collecting is especially damaging.

An ill-advised acquisition example happened a few years ago at the Museum of the City of New York. Given my 16 years of curatorial experience there, which included being responsible for its maritime collections, I am comfortable expressing my alarm about the item in question, which was donated in 2012. It is an ocean-liner deck chair said to be from the ill-fated passenger ship the RMS *Titanic* that sunk in the north Atlantic in 1912 after striking an iceberg. Over 1,500 lives were lost. The ship was heading to New York City on its maiden voyage. I have three questions about the deck chair. One, how can its provenance be certain? Two, how would such a chair survive the sinking? Three, since the ship never made it to New York and the museum is about the history of that city, why on earth was the chair acquired? Research about the acquisition has failed to provide satisfactory answers to my questions. What is revealing is the fact that previous employees immediately responsible for collecting did not want to accept the chair. I was informed that an administrator overrode those objections because the fame of the *Titanic* would garner immediate media attention (which indeed was the case), and the gift was owned and donated by a wealthy member of a famous cosmetic company. Notoriety and wealth are hardly reasons to acquire stuff of no obvious pertinence to a museum.

When collecting, several priorities can dominate: Should a museum emphasize its strengths, fill gaps, or acquire things that will completely alter the institution's collection profile? The stories relayed in this volume cover these options. Four can be easily referred to, though others are relevant too. In Chapter 9, Abantika Parashar tells about acquiring items that reflect the societies in her region of India. These things build and expand upon existing museum collections. Morrison H. Heckscher, in Chapter 4, explains how the Metropolitan Museum of Art filled a significant gap in its expansive collection of decorative arts and design with the purchase of a room designed by Frank Lloyd Wright. In Chapter 3, Jennifer Jankauskas presents how the Montgomery Museum of Fine Art in Alabama is correcting biased collecting practices through intermuseum collaborative acquisition work. In my Chapter 6, I relay the story of getting a huge collection of items for which the Morris Museum in Morristown, New Jersey, was entirely unknown. The Murtogh D. Guinness mechanical musical instruments and automata placed the museum at the international forefront of this once ubiquitous form of entertainment.

In addition to plotting an acquisition course, an issue all museums deal with is the notion of collection quality. Given the breathtaking variety of things found in museums, quality will depend on how a museum seeks to fulfill public service preservation obligations, even if they meet narrow professional opinions. Quality judgments regarding what flora and fauna samples a natural history museum will acquire differ from decisions made by an art or history museum. There are no absolute set guidelines to which all museums must adhere. As a history museum curator, for example, I was perfectly happy to acquire art that might be rejected by an art museum – if the art I wanted was an important visual document of a time, place, event, or person.

Art museums (and the art world at large) used to apply the word *connoisseur* when describing well-qualified people who were responsible for quality when it came to collections. The word has been attacked as fraught with notions of elitism, which in critics' minds counter the democratic wishes museums, at least on the surface, claim to celebrate. Recognizing this current belittling of a once perfectly acceptable approach to museum objects, I suggest connoisseurship is simply misunderstood and suffering from ignorant attacks by dummies who fail to accept the desirability of the elitism they accuse the word to mean in certain applications. If we substitute the words *excellence, knowledge, experience,* and *capable* for the word *elitism*, a lot of analogies support my point. If I hire a plumber, do I want a novice? People servicing my car should be experienced. Why would I have a doctor who fails to be knowledgeable? Do I need a carpenter who is not excellent?

The acquisitions explored in this book resulted from museum staff connoisseurship. Objects were collected for their physical meaning and the need to preserve them in a museological capacity. Whether it is a room designed by Frank Lloyd Wright, a fighter jet, or a collection of regional paintings or bags, the examples discussed are now in museums because people decided those objects represented the best of the best, the crème de la crème, the pinnacle of their kind.

Finally, it is very important to point out that market value was not a reason for any of the museums to collect what is discussed. I used to joke that if asked what something in a particular collection was worth, I'd say, "Nothing." That wisecrack was followed by my explanation that everything a museum owned was priceless. Certainly insurance is in place for collections, but in reality it is impossible to commercially value entire collections, as one would need to follow the market for everything owned. Individual values are assigned to objects when they leave a museum for traveling exhibitions or loans and when sold in a deaccession activity.

Museums are the only public entities that hold three-dimensional material goods for some inherent worth. Knowing why these objects are sought is an excellent way to understand museums. (Any neurological necessity for having museums would be an excellent subject for psychologists to explore and a topic for another publication.) The range of museum collecting approaches described in this volume presents insights about fundamentals museums apply to secure objects of value for all sorts of reasons. Be they history, art, or science museums, they share a singular common existential denominator. All look for what they can use to meet philosophical and practical missions.

Index

Page numbers in *italics* indicate figures. Page numbers followed by n indicate footnotes.

82C Indy Cosworth Car 123–125, *124*
9/11 attacks 105
19th-Century America exhibition 59

Aanischaaukamikw, Cree Native Arts & Crafts Association 39
Aanischaaukamikw Cree Cultural Institute (ACCI) 6, *25*, 40n2; Acquisitions Committee 25–26, 29; acquisitions procedures *26*, 27–30, *28*; Billy Diamond Hall 29; community loans 32–33, *33–34*; Core Collection 31–35, 37–39; Cree Regional Authority (CRA) collection 27, *27*; Eeyou Cree collecting 22–42; Eeyou Istchee Media Collection (EIMC) 34–35; Elders' Project 31–32, *32*; "Featured Object" case 31; "Hommage au chef Billy Diamond" (Bordeleau) 29; "Inspirations from Nature—How the Land Can Inspire Artists" workshops 38; Living Collection 31–35, 37; Rare Books and Special Collections 25–26; "Rediscovering the Tradition of Painted Caribou Coats in Eeyou Istchee" project 35–39, *36*; UNDRIP activation 30–31; "Weejeethoon: African Life Through the Eyes of Canadian Indigenous Peoples" exhibition 33
acquisition (word) 4
acquisitions: by barter 67; case study 35–39; challenge grants for 65–68; co-acquisitions 50–53; common questions 5–6; field 116–120; gifts 72–78, 118–119, *128*, 128–129; methods of collecting 5; museum-defining 79–87; nonverbal history documents 121–136; reasons for success 125, 129, 132, 134; relocations 88–101, *94*; strategies for acquiring art 43–56, 63–78; transfers and transitions 88–101, *94–95*, *97–98*, 134–136, *135*; ways to attract 127–128; *see also specific collections*
acquisition stories 2, 113–120
Air Creebec 29
airplanes, F-16 Fighting Falcon 103–112, *107*
Alston, Robert 100
American Alliance of Museums 2, 106
American Federal-style furniture 132–134, *133*
American Museum of Natural History 5, 137; *Brontosaurus* skeleton 140–141, 144; Hall of Early Dinosaurs 141; Hall of Late Dinosaurs 138; *Tyrannosaurus rex* skeleton 10, 137–144, *138*
Andrews, Gail 45–46, 48, 50–52, 54n3
Annenberg, Walter 72
Antiquities and Art Treasure Act, The, 1972 (India) 116
Apatosaurus 140
Applestein, Dana 68–69
archaeological collections 118
Archives of the History of American Psychology 89
art collections: contemporary art 43–56; outsider art 43; personal 65; strategies for acquisitions 43–56; *see also specific collections*
artists-in-residence 35, 38
Art Loss Register 135

art museums 5, 7, 148–149
Arts Council of Canada 35
art workshops 35, 38–39, 47
Ash Can School 125
Association of Art Museum Directors 51
automata *see* Murtough D. Guinness Collection of Mechanical Musical Instruments
Autumn (Coppedge) 73

Baggy Bear 100
bags: Lee L. Forman Collection of Bags 88–101, *94–98*
Baker, David 92, 101
Baltimore Museum of Art 3–4
Baragwanath, Albert "Barry" 125
Barber's Shop, The (Snell) 67, *67*
barter 67
Baum, Walter 76
Beatles 88, 94
Bennington Museum: *Vermont* (Grandma Moses) 134–136, *135*
Biddle, James 58
Biester, Edward G. 66
Birmingham Museum of Art (BMA) 7, 43–56, 54n4, 148; Collectors Circle for Contemporary Art 45–48; *Old Salem: A Family of Strangers, Series One* (Wilson) 50–53, *52*; *One True Thing: Meditations on Black Aesthetics* exhibition 46–47; *School of Beauty, School of Culture* (Marshall) 44–50, *49*
Blacksmith, Gordon Shecapio 37
Blaton Museum of Art 65
Bloomingdale's 88, 100
Bluebaugh, Marjorie 68
board of trustees 4
Bockroth, Mark 70
Boettcher, Graham 49–50
Bone Cabin Quarry 140–141
bones 137–144, *138*
Bordeleau, Virginia 29
Boscobel Restoration, Inc. (Garrison, New York) 131–133; Boscobel House and Gardens 132–134, *133*; Hudson River School Artists Garden *130*, 130–132
Brontosaurus 140–141, 144
Brown, Barnum ("Mr. Bones") 137–144, *138*
Buckley, Barbara 70–71

Caldwell, Corinne 69–70, 78
Campbell (David P.) Postcard Collection 89
Canada 40n6, 41n15; Eeyou Istchee 6, 22–42, *24*, 40n1
caribou coats: "Rediscovering the Tradition of Painted Caribou Coats in Eeyou Istchee" project (ACCI) 35–39, *36*
"Caribou Universe" series (Mukash) 37
Carnegie Museum of Natural History 140–141
cataloguing 4
Chadbourne, Emily Drane 60
challenge grants 65–66, 68
Chase Bank 87
Christie's 48, 94
Church, Frederick Edwin 132
Ciccarello, Rudy 5
Cleveland 500 Grand Prix 123–125, *124*
co-acquisitions 50–53
collection (word) 4
collections and collecting: community collections 12–21, 113–120; contemporary art 43–56; curator reflections on 20–21; documentation 14–16; Eeyou Cree 22–42, *27*, *32–33*, *36*; field acquisitions 116–120; management strategies 12–21; museum collections 1–11, 145–149; new objects *128*, 128–129; nonverbal history documents 121–136; period rooms 57–62; personal collections 65; private collections 88–101; relocation and ownership change 88–101, *94–95*, *97–98*; removals 2; transfers and transitions 88–101, *94–95*, *97–98*, 134–136, *135*; ways to attract accessions 127–128; *see also specific collections*
collections plan 19–20
commissions 39
community collections: conversions 113–120; field acquisitions 116–120; management strategies 12–21; plans for 19–20; purpose 16–19; references to help make sense of 21; storage 12–14
community loans 32–33, *33–34*
community museums 17, 19–20
computerized records 14
connoisseurship 103, 148–149
Contemporary, The, Baltimore 51
contemporary art 43–56; *see also specific collections*
Coppedge, Fern I. 76; *Autumn* 73
COVID-19 pandemic 43, 119–120
Crawford Auto Aviation Museum 123

152 *Index*

Cree language (Iiyiyiumuwin) 40n1
Cree Nation Government 27, 31, 33
Cree Native Arts & Crafts Association 33
Crozier 93, 100
Cultural Carry-On: America's Literal Baggage exhibition 100
cultural collections: Eeyou Cree 22–42
Cummings (Drs. Nicholas & Dorothy) Center for the History of Psychology 89, *90*; Archives of the History of American Psychology 89; David P. Campbell Postcard Collection 89; *Cultural Carry-On: America's Literal Baggage* exhibition 100; Lee L. Forman Collection of Bags 8–9, 88–101, *94–98*; galleries *91–92*; Institute for Human Sciences & Culture 8–9, 88–101, *94–98*; National Museum of Psychology 89; Oak Native American Ethnographic Collection 89
curators 20–21, 125–128

Dadhara, Lakshimpur 119–120
Davies, Arthur B. 125
deaccessioning 2, 4, 7, 11n4, 19
decolonizing 6–7, 22
Deforest, Robert 58
Desy, Pierrette (Paula) 28
Deubener's 96
D'Harnoncourt, Anne 75
Diamond, Billy 29
digital reference materials 34–35
dinosaurs: *Apatosaurus* 140; *Brontosaurus* 140–141, 144; *Tyrannosaurus rex* 8, 63, 137–144, *138*
District Museum (Jorhat, India) 9, 113–120, *114*
documents: collections management documentation 14–16; nonverbal history document collections 9–10, 121–136
donors and donations 4, 18, 28–29, 100
Douglas, Earl 140–141
Dutta, Hemendra Nath 116–117

Eenou Corporation 33
Eeyou (word) 40n1
Eeyou Cree: ACCI collection 22–42, *27*, *32–33*, *36*; First Snowshoe Walk Ceremony *33*
Eeyou Istchee 22, 40n1; Aanischaaukamikw Cree Cultural Institute (ACCI) 6, 22–42; Eeyou communities 23, *24*; "Rediscovering the Tradition of Painted Caribou Coats in Eeyou Istchee" project (ACCI) 35–39, *36*
Eeyou Istchee Media Collection (EIMC) 34–35
Eight, The 125

F-16 Fighting Falcons 106–107; acquisition 9, 103–112, *107*; Movie Under the Wings project 111–112
Federal Bureau of Investigation 135
Feit, Harvey 28
Feldman, Kaywin 51
Fey, Tina 89
field acquisitions 116–120
Field Museum of Natural History: "Sue" (*Tyrannosaurus rex* skeleton) 8, 63
First Snowshoe Walk Ceremony *33*
Five Angels for the Millennium (Viola) 51
Floating World, The (Michener) 65
Folinsbee, John 76
Forman, Howard 89, 92–93, 100–101
Forman, Lee L. (née Lavinthal) 88
Lee L. Forman Collection of Bags 8–9, 88–101, *94–98*
Francis W. Little House 57–62
Fraser, Brendan 89
funding: challenge grants 65; gifts 72–78, 118–119, *128*, 128–129
furniture: American Federal-style 132–134, *133*; RMS *Titanic* deck chairs 2, 147–148

Gallerie St. Etienne 135–136
Gap-o-sis 125–128
Garber, Daniel 68, 70, 76; *A Wooded Watershed* 68–72, *71*, 74, 78
George, Tina 37
gifts 72–78, 118–119, *128*, 128–129
Glackens, William J. 125
Gordon, Gerald 72
Granger, Walter 140
Great Recession 43
Guinness, Murtogh D. 81–83
Gunner family 29

Harrison, George 94
Hayman, Judy 70
Heckscher, Morrison H. 7, 57–62, 148
Henri, Robert 125
Heritage Park 106, 108
historic house museums 132–134
history museums 5, 122

Hitchcock, Henry-Russell 59
"Hommage au chef Billy Diamond" (Bordeleau) 29
Honolulu Academy of Art 65
Hoving, Tom 60–62
Howe Quarry 143–144
Howe Ranch 142–143
Hudson Bay Company 40n6
Hudson-Fulton Celebration (1909) 58
Hudson River School Artists Garden (Boscobel Restoration, Inc.) *130*, 130–132
Hurst, Carole 73, 75
Huxtable, Ada Louise 62
Hydro Quebec 38

Iiyiyiumuwin (Cree language) 40n1
India: The Antiquities and Art Treasure Act, 1972 116; District Museum (Jorhat, Assam) 9, 113–120, *114*
information technology (IT) 3
Innu/Montagnais nation 29
"Inspirations from Nature—How the Land Can Inspire Artists" workshops 38
Institute for Human Sciences & Culture (University of Akron) 89–92, 100; Lee L. Forman Collection of Bags 8–9, 88–101, *94–98*
interpretive plan 19–20
inventory management 15–16

Jack Shainman Gallery 2014 46
James A. Michener Art Museum 8, 63–78, *64*; *Autumn* (Coppedge) *73*; *The Pigs and the Crow* (Nordfeldt) *75*; Putman/Smith Gallery 70–72, 74; *Rooftops, New Hope* (Miller) *77*; *The Trout Brook* (Redfield) *74*, 75; *Untitled* (Night Snow Scene) (Sotter) *76*; *A Wooded Watershed* (Garber) 68–72, *71*, 74
Jankauskas, Jennifer 7, 43–56, 148
J.B. Henderson Construction 109–110
John Dinkeloo Associates 61
Jorhat, India District Museum 9, 113–120, *114*

Kachamari Pathar, Golaghat 116–118
Kallir, Otto 135
Katsiff, Bruce 8, 63–78
Kaufman, Jason Edward 51
Kearns, Jodi 8–9, 88–101
Kelly, Drye and Warren 82
Kent, Henry Watson 58

Kirtland Air Force Base (Albuquerque, New Mexico) 104, 107, 109
Kraushaar, Antoinette *126*, 127
K'Taqmkuk Mi'kmaq Historical Museum 29

Lafayette, The (Sloan) 125–128, *126*
Lathrop, William 76
Lawson, Ernest 125
Leiby, D. Kenneth 66–67
Lenfest, Gerry and Marguerite 72–78
Lennon, John 94
Lewis, Craig 70
Lightcap, Alan *86*
Little, Francis W.: Northome (Wright) 8, 57–62, 148
Lockheed Martin Corp. 104
Los Angeles County Museum of Art 46
Lost Boys, The (Marshall) 48
Louise F. Dow Co. 96
Louvre 8, 63
Loveness, Don 59–60
Luks, George 125

MAACM (Museum of American Arts & Crafts Movement) 5
Mackenzie, Marguerite 28
Mahuramukh, Golaghat 118–119
makaahiikan 41n14
Marsh, Othniel C. 139–141
Marshall, Kerry James 46; *Kerry James Marshall: Mastry* exhibition 46; *The Lost Boys,* 1993 48; *One True Thing: Meditations on Black Aesthetics* exhibition 46–47; *School of Beauty, School of Culture,* 2012 44–50, *49*; *Vignette,* 2003 48
Martin, Syd and Sharon 76–77
Martino, Antonio 76
Maryland Historical Society 51
Mayer, Grace 125
McCartney, Paul 94
mechanical musical instruments: Murtough D. Guinness Collection of Mechanical Musical Instruments 79–87, *80*, *86*, 148
media acquisitions 34
Memphis Brooks Museum of Art, Tennessee 51–52
Menarick, Paula: Painted Caribou Hide by Margaret Orr, Paula Menarick, Cree-Lynn Shecapio, and Emily Sam (2020.07.01) 39
Mercer Museum 63–64, 78
metadata 93–100

Metropolitan Museum of Art 46, 82, 85, 148; *19th-Century America* exhibition 59; American Bicentennial Wing 61; American Wing 7, 57–60; *Kerry James Marshall: Mastry* exhibition 46; Northome (Wright) living room 57–62; Trustee Acquisition Committee 61
Michener, James A. (Jim) 64–65, 78; *The Floating World* 65; Michener Endowment Challenge 66, 78
Michener Endowment Challenge 66, 78
military acquisitions: F-16 Fighting Falcon 103–112, *107*
Miller, R. A. D.: *Rooftops, New Hope* 77
Miller, Steven 1–11, 79–87, 121–136, 145–149
Mining the Museum (Wilson) 51
mission statement 17
Morris Museum (Morristown, New Jersey) 8, 79, 81, 148; Murtough D. Guinness Collection of Mechanical Musical Instruments 79–87, *80*, *86*
Moses, Anna Mary Robertson (Grandma Moses) 134–135; *Vermont* 134–136, *135*
Movie Under the Wings project 111–112
Mukash, Natasia: Artwork by Natasia Mukash (2020.05.01-.02) 37; "Caribou Universe" series 37
Murtough D. Guinness Collection of Mechanical Musical Instruments 79–87, *80*, *86*, 148
museum collections 1–11, 145–149; acquisition stories 2, 113–120; strategies for management of 12–21; *see also specific museums and collections*
museum-defining acquisitions 79–87
Museum of American Arts & Crafts Movement (MAACM) 5
Museum of Bags 88–101, *94*
Museum of Contemporary Art, Los Angeles: *Kerry James Marshall: Mastry* exhibition 46
Museum of Contemporary Art Chicago 46
Museum of Early Southern Decorative Arts, Winston-Salem 51–52
Museum of Fine Arts, Boston 85
Museum of Modern Art, New York 46
Museum of the City of New York 2, 84, 124, 147–148; *The Lafayette* (Sloan) 125–128, *126*; *Yonah Shimmel Knish Bakery* (Pagremanski) *128*, 128–129
museums: areas of specialty 5; art museums 5, 7, 148–149; board of trustees 4; collecting policies 2; common questions when collecting 5–6; community museums 17, 19–20; core purpose 1; decolonizing 22; definition 4, 8; historic house museums 132–134; history museums 5, 122; mission statement 17, 19–20; as object libraries 4; as research library 9–10; retention commitment 2; science museums 5; science technology museums 5; trustees 4; *see also specific museums by name*
musical instruments: Murtough D. Guinness Collection of Mechanical Musical Instruments 79–87, *80*, *86*, 148

Naskapi nation 29
National Atomic Museum 104
National Environmental Protection Act (NEPA) 109
National Gallery of Art, Washington, D.C. 46, 51
National Museum of Nuclear Science & History 104–106; F-16 Fighting Falcon acquisition 9, 103–112, *107*; Movie Under the Wings project 111–112
National Museum of Psychology 89
National Music Museum (Vermilion, South Dakota) 85
Newark Museum, Newark, New Jersey 4
New Hope Modernists 77
Newington Cropsey Foundation (Hastings-on-Hudson, New York) 131–132
New Mexico Air National Guard (NMANG) 106–108, 111–112
new objects *128*, 128–129
Noble, Joseph Veach 125
nonverbal history documents 9–10, 121–136
Nordfeldt, Bror Julius: *The Pigs and the Crow* 75
Northome (Wright) 8, 57–62, 148
numbering systems 14

Oak Native American Ethnographic Collection 89
Oberholtzer, Cath 28
O'Brien, Conan 89
Old Salem: A Family of Strangers, Series One (Wilson) 50–53, *52*
One True Thing: Meditations on Black Aesthetics exhibition 46–47
Orr, Margaret: Artwork (2019.13.01 ab; 2019.13.02) 38; Contemporary

Creations (2020.06.01-.02ab) 38–39; Painted Caribou Hide by Margaret Orr, Paula Menarick, Cree-Lynn Shecapio, and Emily Sam (2020.07.01) 39
Osborn, Henry Fairfield 139–141, 144
Ouje-Bougoumou Cree Nation 6, 37
Ouje-Bougoumou Justice Department 39
outsider art 43

Pagremanski, Hedy 129; *Yonah Shimmel Knish Bakery 128*, 128–129
painted caribou coats: "Rediscovering the Tradition of Painted Caribou Coats in Eeyou Istchee" project (ACCI) 35–39, *36*
paleontology 137–144, *138*
PandaMania 100
Parashar, Abantika 9, 113–120, 148
Past/Future (Mukash) 37
Pennsylvania Building, 1926 Sesquicentennial Celebration 68
Pennsylvania Impressionists 63–78
Pennsylvania Museum of Art (PMA) 73–74
Pennsylvania State University, Mt. Alto: Garber scholarship fund 70; State Forestry School 68–70
period rooms 57–62
Petersen, Roy 72
Peterson, Brian 73
Philadelphia Museum of Art (PMA) 4, 72
photographs 34, 93–100
Phyfe, Duncan *133*
Pigs and the Crow, The (Nordfeldt) 75
Polaroids (Warhol) 48
Polis, Malcolm 72
Pompidou Center, Paris 51
portraits, posthumous 130–132
Predergast, Maurice 125
Preston, Douglas J. 10, 137–144
Preston, Richard 28
prices 50, 149

racing cars 123–125, *124*
Rayhal, Bobby 123; 82C Indy Cosworth Car 123–125, *124*
reaccessioning 19
recordkeeping 14–16, 136
Redfield, Edward W. 76; *The Trout Brook 74*, 75
"Rediscovering the Tradition of Painted Caribou Coats in Eeyou Istchee" project (ACCI) 35–37, *36*; Antler Bone and Painting Tools (2019.16.01-.08) 37;

Artwork by Margaret Orr (2019.13.01 ab; 2019.13.02) 38; Artwork by Natasia Mukash (2020.05.01-.02) 37; Artwork by Tim Whiskeychan (2019.02.01-.04; 2019.03.01-.86) 37; Contemporary Creations by Margaret Orr (2020.06.01-.02ab) 38–39; Painted Caribou Hide by Margaret Orr, Paula Menarick, Cree-Lynn Shecapio, and Emily Sam (2020.07.01) 39; Painted Hide Samplers (2019.17.01-.02) 37; Prepared Caribou Hide (2019.15.1) 37
Reflection (Mukash) 37
relocations 88–101, *94*
research workshops 39
retention commitment 2
Richardson, H.H. 59
Ripley, Vaughn 100
RMS *Titanic* 2, 147–148
Robinon, Edward 58
Roche, Kevin 61
Rooftops, New Hope (Miller) *77*
Rosen, Charles 76
Rosenblatt, Arthur 59, 61
Rupert's Land 40n6
Ryder, Jere 85
Ryder, Stephen 79–83

Sam, Emily: Painted Caribou Hide by Margaret Orr, Paula Menarick, Cree-Lynn Shecapio, and Emily Sam (2020.07.01) 39
Sandia National Labs 104, 109
Sankofa Society: Friends of African American and African Art 48, 54n4
School of Beauty, School of Culture (Marshall) 44–50, *49*
science museums 5
science technology museums 5
security 4
Semingson, Diane 70
Shainman, Jack 47
Shannon, Molly 89
Shecapio, Cree-Lynn: Painted Caribou Hide by Margaret Orr, Paula Menarick, Cree-Lynn Shecapio, and Emily Sam (2020.07.01) 39
Shinn, Everett 125
Sinclair Oil Company 142
Singh, Sh. Nikunja 116–117
Sloan, John 125, 127; *The Lafayette* 125–128, *126*
Smith, Carolyn 68–69

Smithsonian Institution 8, 63
Snell, Henry 67; *The Barber's Shop* 67, *67*
Soloway, Carl 51
Sotter, George W. 76; *Untitled* (Night Snow Scene) *76*
Sozanski, Edward 66
Spanogiannis, Mike 94
Spencer, Robert 76
Starr, Ringo 94
Stevenson, Mr. and Mrs. Raymond V. 59–62
storage 12–14
storage shelving 93, *95*, *97*
Suburban Cable 72–73
"Sue" (*Tyrannosaurus rex* skeleton) 8, 63
Sullivan, Louis 59
Summers, John 6, 12–21

Tafel, Edgar 59–60
Tanner, Adrian 28
Tate Modern, London 51
technical areas 109
Titanic see RMS *Titanic*
Tracy, Berry B. 59–60
transfers and transitions: Lee L. Forman Collection of Bags 88–101, *94–98*; *Vermont* (Grandma Moses) 134–136, *135*
Trout Brook, The (Redfield) *74*, 75
trustees 4
Two Red Roses Foundation 5
Tyrannosaurus rex: American Museum of Natural History skeletons 10, 137–144, *138*; Field Museum of Natural History skeleton ("Sue") 8, 63

Ugalde, Fran 8–9, 88–101
Ukiyo-e prints 65
United Nations Declaration on the Rights of Indigenous Peoples (UNDRIP) 30–31
United States 4
University of Akron, Ohio: *Cultural Carry-On: America's Literal Baggage* exhibition 100; Drs. Nicholas & Dorothy Cummings Center for the History of Psychology 8–9, 88–101, *90–92*, *94–98*; Institute for Human Sciences & Culture 8–9, 88–101, *94–98*
University of Texas at Austin: Blaton Museum of Art 65

Untitled (Night Snow Scene) (Sotter) *76*
U.S. Air Force 104–105, 108
U.S. Department of Energy 104–105
U.S. Department of the Environment 107–108

Velthuis, Olav 44
Vermont (Grandma Moses) 134–136, *135*
Vienna Secession (Austria) 49
Vignette (Marshall) 48
Viola, Bill: *Five Angels for the Millennium* 51

Walken, Christopher 89
Walker, Kara 50
Walker Art Center, Minneapolis 46
Walther, James (Jim) 9, 103–112
Warhol, Andy 48, 88
Washington Redskins *98*
Waskaganish Cree Nation 29
"Weejeethoon: African Life Through the Eyes of Canadian Indigenous Peoples" exhibition (ACCI) 33
Weems, Carrie Mae 50
Weinstein, Elaine 92, 100
Western Reserve Historical Society (Cleveland, Ohio) 79, 83, 123; 82C Indy Cosworth Car 123–125, *124*
Whapmagoostui Cree Nation 37
Whiskeychan, Tim: Artwork (2019.02.01-.04; 2019.03.01-.86) 38
Whitman, Robert 135–136
Whitney Museum of American Art, New York 51
Williston, Samuel 139
Wilson, Fred 51; *Mining the Museum* 51; *Old Salem: A Family of Strangers, Series One,* 1995 50–53, *52*
Wooded Watershed, A (Garber) 68–72, *71*, 74
workshops 35, 38–39, 47
works in progress 100–101
Wright, Frank Lloyd 59; Northome (Francis W. Little house) 8, 57–62, 148
Wyatt, Greg *130*, 131

Yale Museum 140
Yonah Shimmel Knish Bakery (Pagremanski) *128*, 128–129
Young Canada Works 35

For Product Safety Concerns and Information please contact our EU
representative GPSR@taylorandfrancis.com
Taylor & Francis Verlag GmbH, Kaufingerstraße 24, 80331 München, Germany

www.ingramcontent.com/pod-product-compliance
Lightning Source LLC
Chambersburg PA
CBHW050302010526
44108CB00040B/2108